IMAGES
of England

CENTRAL
SHEFFIELD

Laying the telephone cable, Norfolk Street, 1887. Highways Department staff are taking the opportunity to carry out routine repairs to gritstone setts and granite curbstones. The shops were opposite the junction with Norfolk Row, between the Assembly Rooms (page 56) and Hays' Wine Vaults, which now house the Ruskin Museum. G.R. Boyd was a tailor, Sarah Shaw kept a spice shop, and Henry Priestley, on the right, was a chemist. Upper Norfolk Street was to be the testing ground for Col Bingham's patent wood paving (see page 159).

IMAGES
of England

CENTRAL
SHEFFIELD

Compiled by
Martin Olive

TEMPUS

First published 1994
Reprinted 1994, 1995, 1998, 1999
Copyright © Martin Olive, 1994

Tempus Publishing Limited
The Mill, Brimscombe Port, Stroud,
Gloucestershire GL5 2QG

ISBN 0 7524 0011 8

Typesetting and origination
Tempus Publishing Limited
Printed in Great Britain by
Midway Clark Printing, Wiltshire

Dedicated to my former colleagues
Jo Lambert
and
Mary Walton
for their services to the local history of Sheffield

Contents

Acknowledgements

This compilation has been made possible through the help and goodwill of many people over many years. Some I have never known, others, sadly, have passed away, and many more have moved home; I offer apologies to those I have been unable to contact. To the people in the following list, and many others inevitably omitted, I am deeply grateful.

All who have collected photographs and given or lent them to the Local Studies Library, including: Mr and Mrs Alsopp, Mr T.R. Arkell, Jill Beebe, Mr H. Bradley, Brightside and Carbrook Co-operative Society, Mr R.B. Clark, Mr V. Golightly, Mr Green, Mr J.B. Himsworth, The Holberry Society, Mr C.H. Lea, Mr H. Lovatt, Miss Lucas, Mr Marshman, Mr V. Mercer, Mr R. Moore, Daniel O'Neill and Sons, Miss Jill Platts, Mr Tom Pountney, Miss Grace Preston, Mr H. Richardson, the *Sheffield Telegraph*, Mr D.J. Smith, Mr F.W. Smith, Mr R.S. Smith, Mr J. Saddington, Mr A.B. Stables, Mrs Shaw, T.W. Ward Ltd, Wilks Bros, Mrs Wooding.

The Library Staff, especially my former colleagues in the Local Studies Library: Maureen Bailey, Pat Clark, Alison Cooper, Doug Hindmarch, Sue Hulse, Sue Linton, Helen Purves, Sylvia Pybus and Mike Spick, who look after the photographs, mount them, catalogue them and store them and will (one day) have them all in a computer so they will pop up at the touch of a button; also Cynthia Woodhouse in the Photographic Department who has made the copies and is responsible for keeping the photographic survey up to date. The ratepayers of Sheffield, without whose support there would be no collection.

On a personal note I would especially like to thank Doug Hindmarch and his staff in Local Studies for their help and patience; likewise Cynthia Woodhouse for her photography. George Rogerson has kindly undertaken the typing and proffered much constructive criticism.

Introduction

The photographs in this book have been selected from more than 60,000 in the picture collection maintained by the Local Studies Library in the Central Library in Surrey Street. This collection forms a visual record of Sheffield since the earliest days of photography, and it is to be hoped that Sheffielders in future will be able to enjoy a similar record of the city we know today, and react to our strange doings with the appropriate shock, amusement or nostalgia. The collection could only have come about through donations, bequests and temporary loans to enable the Library's photographic staff to make copies. One of the objects of this book is to encourage Sheffielders and ex-Sheffielders to continue to support the collection. If you have or know of any old photographs of Sheffield the Local Studies Library would be delighted to hear from you.

Because of the size of the collection I have restricted the scope of this book geographically and in time. All the photographs were taken within a mile of the Market Place (alias Castle Square, until very recently the Hole-in-the-Road) which has been the centre of the town for at least six centuries, and is about to be born again as a Supertram station. At the dawn of photography three square miles easily encompassed the entire urban area, and included parts of the Park which still resembled a noble country estate. During Victoria's reign the town expanded rapidly and the select- ion excludes the great steel works in the East End, while in the west it stops just short of those two well-loved institutions on Western Bank and Bramall Lane. In time the photographs cover about a century from 1850. The book leaves Sheffield on the brink of becoming an engineer's dream in concrete, with soaring tower blocks, inner ring roads and pedestrian underpasses. Perhaps this age has now been symbolically closed with the rubble from Hyde Park Flats being used to fill in the Hole-in-the-Road, but this is another story. Each section in this book covers a geographical area, except for the final section, which concentrates on the traditional light metal trades. These were carried on in workshops widely scattered through the City Centre, and in some cases it is not possible to find a precise location for each photograph.

Though photographs offer a fascinating insight into the life of a hundred years ago, the picture they present is inevitably incomplete and distorted. The earliest professional photographers made their living out of portraits, which usually depicted middle-class people in their Sunday best inside a studio. When amateurs ventured outside, it was usually to lug their apparatus out to the more picturesque suburbs or over the hill to the Peak District. The main exceptions were Theophilus Smith, a monumental mason and medieval scholar who published a series of local views in 1862, and Arthur Hayball, whose views from his house on Hanover Street in the mid-1850s are probably the oldest surviving photographs of Sheffield. Eight out of ten early views of the area were taken in the immediate aftermath of the Great Sheffield Flood of 1864, but curiously none seems to have been taken in the town centre. In 1875 the Corporation took powers to widen many of the central streets. The process took more than twenty five years and allowed time for photographers to record many of the historic buildings which were destroyed in the improvements, before returning to celebrate the new ones. Some activities provided attractive and willing subjects for the camera. The Fire Brigade, for example, seem to have been obsessed with having their picture taken. The great steel works were pioneer users of industrial photography, but were mostly located outside the town centre. By the turn of the century the Mottershaw Brothers and H. Jasper Redfern, best known as pioneers of cinematography, were commissioned for publicity work, and many City Centre views were produced by postcard firms. Although the collection well reflects the public and commercial side of the City Centre life, it seldom penetrates far into the activities of most of its residents, who were poor, did not have cameras and were highly suspicious of visiting photographers. Most of the pictures of Sheffield slums were taken just before they were demolished and the inhabitants were in cheerful mood at the prospect of a council house. Any picture of washing day in a Sheffield court would be of great interest. A rich sporting and recreational life focused on public houses and has seldom been recorded. Pubs were much photographed even in Victorian times, but you would be hard put to find visual evidence of anybody actually drinking in one. A local newspaper which published photographs of old Sheffield in the 1930s employed a useful general purpose caption which read: "This Photograph offers another fascinating glimpse of a Sheffield which has long gone. Exactly where these buildings stood we cannot say, but they certainly look old." Much as I admire the editor's discretion, I feel I am expected to stick my neck out a little further. Some of the information is surmise; I can only plead that it is reasonably based. Most pictures arrived in the collection with some means of identifying the subject but much less often the date. Internal evidence on the photograph, such as names on shops or pubs and dates on posters can be checked against street directories. Ordnance Survey plans are useful for long forgotten minor streets and back yards. Events depicted in photographs can be checked in local newspapers, where they were often chronicled in overwhelming detail. There remain some puzzles and frustrations. Copies of the same print often turn up from different sources, sometimes with contradictory identifications. Elaborate circumstantial oral information is sometimes called in question by documentary evidence. I have excluded one or two photographs which have left me totally baffled; in other captions the words "perhaps" or "probably" should no doubt appear more frequently than they do. Anybody who can correct or add to information on an ancestor or an ancestral haunt is very welcome to do so. Most of the photographers have to remain anonymous. Some of their names occur in the acknowledgements, but donors of prints were not necessarily photographers and it is evident that circulation and copying of negatives was taking place from an early period. This practice ensured the survival of images but left the identity of the original photographer in doubt. Photographers also tended to be attracted to the same view points at the same time but further infomation would again be welcome. This book will have served its purpose if readers are able to share some of the pleasure I have derived from a long association with the picture collection in the Local Studies Library. I also hope it encourages Sheffielders to explore the collection for themselves and to lend any similar prints which they may have so that they can be copied and made available to their fellow citizens now and in the future.

One

High Street, Fargate

High Street, Fargate. High Street linked the medieval market with the Parish Church. Fargate was the way leading out of town towards the south. In the seventeenth century there were farms and cottages with gardens; a few had smithies in their back yards. By the end of the century timber framed buildings with thatched roofs began to give way to ones of stone or brick covered with grey slates, but this was a slow process as some of the Victorian photographs show. Retail shops developed in the mid-eighteenth century. A century later Cole Brothers opened the first department store on the corner of Fargate and Church Street, with an iron frame, plate glass windows and an upstairs sales floor. All this time High Street and Fargate remained no more than their medieval width. Plans for widening were included in the 1875 Corporation improvement scheme, but long delayed. Work began on Fargate in the 'eighties, but the shop keepers on High Street held out until 1895. One result of the delay was a comprehensive photographic record of the improvements. Unfortunately many of the proud new buildings on the south side of High Street were devastated by the Blitz. On Fargate developers have had much the same effect.

High Street 1862 from the junction of Church Street and Fargate, a view taken by Theophilus Smith. On the left are the Parish Church Gates, with Pawson and Brailsford's shop behind. High Street is no wider than it was in the Middle Ages and apart from Fosters' on the right no building is more than three storeys high. The end of the Fitzalan Market Hall can just be seen in the distance.

The same view nearly fifty years later from a slightly lower angle. By demolishing all the buildings on the right hand side the street has been more than doubled in width and the new buildings on that side are of a style more befitting the status of a city of 440,000 inhabitants. On the left progress is less marked.

Ebenezer Elliott, the Corn Law Rhymer, overlooks the Market Place from the front of Fitzalan Market in the early 1870s. High Street is on the left. It is evidently early morning; coal carts are delivering and the apparent absence of people is belied by the shadows of those who have passed too quickly to be recorded by the camera. Elliott's statue was erected by subscription in 1854 and was moved to Weston Park when it opened in 1875, starting a trend for the migration of statues from the City Centre to the suburbs.

The south side of High Street from Coles' Corner, c.1895, before the long anticipated widening got under way. There was prolonged wrangling between the Corporation and the property owners over whether the widening would do them a favour by improving access or ruin them by depriving them of floor space. In the event the larger businesses, notably Fosters and John Walsh, did very well out of the compensation money. At busy times the street was dangerously narrow for traffic and tramways were banned from the centre of town until High Street had been widened. The buildings on the right had been the White Bear Inn, where the Archbishop of York lodged on official visits to Sheffield in the eighteenth century. The three-horse bus is on the hilly route to Broomhill.

Lower High Street opposite the Market Place c.1895, with improvements in progress. The picture shows the entrance to Change Alley, a street which has been swept away by Arundel Gate. The wooden framed shop had been a substantial town house and it has been suggested that it was one built by the Earl of Shrewsbury's bailiff in 1574. The tall building beyond is the King's Head.

A side view of the King's Head c.1895 from Change Alley. It was one of the leading inns of the town. From 1745 to 1768 the owner and licencee was Leonard Webster, a Town Trustee who was wealthy and powerfully connected. In his day there was a bowling green in front of the inn, but he used the land to construct Change Alley. This resulted in a cramped approach to the main entrance. Nevertheless, under William Wright (landlord 1768-81) it rivalled the Angel as the leading Sheffield coaching inn. It was rebuilt in 1896 only to be destroyed in the Blitz.

A closer view of the shops on the south side of High Street, c.1895. The buildings on the right have been removed and the basement used as an extension to Fosters', whose clearance sale lasted many months. The domed Grand Clothing Hall was originally the Post Office and once sported classical columns facing the street and a statue of Mercury in place of the curious crowning ventilator. The facades of the new south side of High Street were already rising behind these buildings. In 1896 the old buildings were torn down and the full glory of their High Victorian replacements was revealed.

Pawson and Brailsford's stationery shop at the Church Gates, top of High Street, 1883. The completed half of the new building towers above the surviving half of the old. Pawson and Brailsford had an extensive business in commercial printing and their colour lithography had a national reputation. Their new premises, also known as Parade Chambers, brought in good rents accommodating solicitors and accountants on the upper storeys above the shops. The renaissance trimmings and ecclesiastical details – note especially the gargoyles – acknowledged the Parish Church next door and the status of Henry Pawson as Churchwarden. It was fifteen years before any other building of such size and ambition appeared on High Street.

The south side of High Street c.1905, with the new buildings revealed. George Street leads off in front of Hope Brothers. The new shops include two hotels with restaurants; all of the rest sell clothing of some description. Only Fosters' Building on the extreme right, occupied by Harrisons, survived the Blitz or its immediate aftermath.

John Walsh's department store on High Street soon after it opened in 1900. John Walsh was a native of County Limerick and learned his trade at Cockaynes' in Angel Street. In 1875 he opened his own modest shop selling baby linen and ladies' outfitting on the north side of High Street. The Corporation's High Street widening scheme proved his great opportunity as he had been busy acquiring property on either side of the street. At street level his new building was all steel and glass, but on the upper floors this functional skeleton was disguised in traditional Huddersfield stone. The top floors were dormitories for staff. John Walsh was a Roman Catholic and it was a comfort to mothers of that religion to know that their daughters would be spared from meat on Fridays and turned out on Holy Days for early Mass at St Marie's. By 1925 there were six hundred employees, including those in house removals, decorating and cabinet making. The building was burnt out in the Blitz but the business returned to new premises on the same site and is now owned by House of Fraser.

Opposite: The north side of High Street c.1905 from Walsh's windows. John Walsh had also been responsible for Central Chambers and High Court immediately across the street. Between these modern buildings and Parade Chambers stretches a row of unimproved buildings serving a variety of purposes from newspaper offices to photographers, tea merchants, hairdressers and an India rubber goods shop.

Market Place, looking down Angel Street c.1898, showing one of the Duke of Norfolk's ornamental gas lamps which were displaced by the electric trams. On the right is Cockaynes' department store with its new glass fronted arcade which was added in 1897. T.B. and W. Cockayne were born in Sheffield of a Derbyshire family and had opened their draper's shop on the same site in 1829. In the 1920s male staff still wore morning dress and floor walkers dressed in coat and tails. Pay depended on commission, but money could be saved by living in and sporting and social activities were subsidized. H.L.Brown, the jeweller next door, came from Warsaw as a refugee after the 1860 uprising. His Polish employers had been agents for Sheffield cutlery. He became a conspicuously patriotic Englishman as well as a strong support to the local Jewish community. His firm providentially moved from Market Place before the Blitz.

Looking down the east side of Angel Street from the Market Place c.1895, showing the corner of Fitzalan Market Hall on the right with King Street beyond. The cupola of the Old Town Hall (now the County Court) can be seen on the right background.

Devastation on Angel Street after the Blitz in December, 1940. Cockaynes' was a total loss, though subsequently rebuilt on the same site. Surprisingly, Syminton and Croft on the right, at the top of King Street, was temporarily patched up and returned to business.

The Marples Hotel c.1930, on the corner of High Street and Fitzalan Square. The replacement King's Head Hotel is on the right. Fisher Son and Sibray, the Handsworth nurserymen and hardware dealers, had the old established shop next door in Fitzalan Square.

Extracting a victim from the vaults of the Marples Hotel, 13 December 1940. The Marples had put on special entertainments for war workers and when the sirens sounded a crowded house had made its way to the cellars. After the building collapsed on top of them it was a long time before rescuers could dig them out. Seventy people suffocated and only seven were brought out alive.

High Street from Coles' windows after the Blitz, 1943. The view is similar to the ones on page 10. The most notable addition is Kelmsley House on the left, completed in 1913, apparently reluctant to advertise its presence. The Blitz spared the older shops on the north side, but left widespread devastation beyond Fosters' Building on the right, and Burton's at the end remained an empty shell till finally demolished in 1960.

Coles' Corner in 1930, from the windows of Kelmsley House. The view was taken to show lunch hour crowds in Fargate. Pedestrians are as usual paying little attention to the policeman on point duty. This was the crossing of the main roads from Leeds to Exeter and Lincoln to Manchester, but there was still plenty of room to park. Belisha beacons were afterwards installed.

Fargate, looking towards High Street in 1886. On the left at the end is Cole Brothers' department store, which started on the corner with Church Street in 1869 and gradually spread back along Fargate. The only modern building on the right was The Exchange Drapery Stores.

Tuckwood's grocery stores on Fargate, c.1930. Note the chairs provided for customers. J.J.G. Tuckwood took over the Exchange Drapery Stores in 1887 and moved his Great Northern Grocery Stores there from across the street. From the first the new store incorporated a restaurant. The firm was taken over by Atkinson's in 1946 and the restaurant was transferred to Surrey Street.

The Assay Office was established by Act of Parliament in 1773 and proved crucial to the development of the silver trades in the town. This building with the Lion over the door was built for the Office on the south of Fargate in 1795. In 1881 it was demolished to make way for New Surrey Street and the Assay Office moved to Leopold Street.

A summer afternoon in Fargate c.1925, with straw hats in evidence and blinds drawn on the sunny side. The Telegraph Building (Kelmsley House) provided a familiar landmark in place of a row of undistinguished shops.

From the Town Hall tower, looking over Fargate towards the Parish Church, c.1908. Prominent behind the Green Dragon Hotel is the rear of the Cutlers' Company's upper Banqueting Hall. Beyond Church Street on the left can be seen the Gladstone Buildings. Among other details visible from this height readers may like to pick out the chimney of the engine which provided power and lighting to the *Sheffield Telegraph*. The curiously prom- inent building behind the Parish Church is Robertshaws' printing works on St Peter's Close.

Two

Castle and Markets

Sheffield Castle was very efficiently demolished by order of Parliament in 1648. It has left no visual record and few physical remains. Like the Castle, the Markets belonged to the Lords of Sheffield and in the Middle Ages did more then anything else to bring prosperity to the town. There was a market cross in the Market Place and another, the "Irish" cross, at the foot of Angel Street. Up to the eighteenth century animals were sold in the Haymarket (then known as the Bullstake) and slaughtered across the road (now Fitzalan Square). On market days stalls for meat, fruit and vegetables spread out from the Market Place and filled the High Street and Angel Street. In 1874 the Duke of Norfolk built a new market hall at the bottom of High Street. Animals were now sold in the Wicker and slaughtered on the site of the old Castle. In the 1850s the Norfolk Market Hall was built on Haymarket and the existing one on High Street was enlarged. The City Council purchased the ancient market rights in 1899 from the Duke of Norfolk, transferred the slaughter houses from Castle Hill to Cricket Inn Road, and built the new Castle Market in their place. Since 1968 the old market place has been designated Castle Square (otherwise the Hole-in-the-Road) while the modern markets occupy the site of the Castle.

The Angel Hotel, Angel Street, c.1935, a leading Sheffield inn in the eighteenth century. From 1728-1762 a theatre flourished in the inn yard, and the first stage coach to London left in 1760. In 1862 they were still advertising a livery and bait stables, offering post horses, wedding and party carriages, omnibuses for pleasure excursions and all the necessaries for funerals. The inn was rebuilt in 1816 on the original site and a feature of the rebuilding was this terracotta angel made by the sculptor Rossi, who was lodging across the road. The Angel was totally destroyed in the Blitz.

Looking down Angel Street c.1930, with Snig Hill at the bottom, Cockaynes' and the Angel on the left and Muddiman's Buildings on the right (later Syminton and Croft). Contrasts between modish and traditional dress styles will be noted.

Looking down Angel Street from the roof of the burnt-out Walsh's in 1943, showing the effects of the Blitz. Burton's building on the right is an empty skeleton and only a stump of Syminton and Croft's survives, windows blacked out but still selling drapery. Castle Street is revealed behind with the tower of the Law Courts, Tennants' Brewery chimney and, on the far right, the Royal Victoria Hotel. In the centre of the horizon can be seen the spire of Sir John Brown's Church on Ellesmere Road.

Snig Hill from the crossing of Bank Street and Castle Street, c.1893. The *Sheffield Independent* newspaper still owned the former printing offices on Bank Street corner, though it had not been printed there since 1862 and they were let to a dentist.

Snig Hill from West Bar, shortly before the shops on the left hand side were demolished in 1900. Hoveys' new store stands at the top on the corner of Castle Street. Boots' first Sheffield branch was established in nondescript premises on the left and moved to its present position on High Street in 1900.

The Pack Horse Hotel at the bottom of Snig Hill, with old buildings in course of demolition, 1900. The Packhorse had been built in 1846 as the show pub for Chambers and Co.'s Bridge Street Brewery nearby, but they were soon taken over by Thomas Berry's of Moorhead. Political meetings used to be addressed from the balcony, and in latter years boxing took place in a room at the back. The hotel was pulled down in 1904.

Picturesque but very ramshackle shops at the bottom of Snig Hill, cleared in 1900 and replaced by Corporation flats. Relics of a time when Sheffield's town houses were mostly timber framed, they were much painted and photographed in their last years.

Castle Street loking across Haymarket into Exchange Street, c.1905.

Sale of ladies' shoes to mark the reopening of the Brightside and Co-op in temporary premises, 1950. After the destruction of the City Stores in the Blitz they moved to the corner of Angel Street and Castle Street, where Castle House eventually took shape. In austerity Sheffield customers are happy to queue for goods in short supply.

Mr Charles Henry Cleathero in the doorway of his tailoring establishment, one of the distinctive wooden shop fronts below the Court House in Waingate, c.1902. Mr Cleathero had served with Ormrod and Faulkner of Angel Street and lived on Fowler Street at Wincobank where he also kept the Engineer's Hotel.

Waingate from the Haymarket in the 1920s. A young pedestrian is being trained to wait for the policeman before crossing. The buildings across the road are new. The Brightside and Carbrook City Stores were extended upwards two storeys in 1930.

Police and traffic at the foot of Waingate, c.1890. The Royal Hotel was opened in 1779 as the Reindeer with a literal flourish of trumpets, and changed its name several times before settling down as the Royal in 1841. Its furnishings, as reported in 1913 when it was demolished, included a spit driven by a water wheel.

A seller of baskets, mats and plaited horse whips doggedly solicits the custom of a group of schoolboys in the Haymarket, c.1900. The Norfolk Market Hall, which the Corporation had just purchased from the Duke of Norfolk, is in the right background. Tramway equipment is in evidence, but horse omnibuses have not yet been restricted to the outer suburbs.

Opposite: William Henry Haigh's Broomhill omnibus pulls up Haymarket in 1890. The profitable Broomhill route was hotly contested by rival omnibus proprietors and at midday on 14 July Haigh pulled out of the service in a huff rather than share it with Reuben Thompson. He was already facing court action over an accident to one of his buses which had been speeding down Glossop Road without driver or conductor.

Inside the Norfolk Market Hall, c.1906. L. and A. Wilkinson were owned by James Wilkinson of Birkendale and advertised themselves as booksellers, stationers, printers and bookbinders. They were also early agents for Edison's phonographs and records.

N. Smith and Sons' toy stall in the body of Norfolk Market Hall, c.1933. The assistants are Ivy Moore, Irene Ollerenshaw, Yvette Pratt, Margaret Deanaley and Jessie Humphries.

From the roof of Davy's restaurant on Haymarket, looking towards the Royal Victoria Hotel before the area was redeveloped in 1914-20. The view is of historical interest as it shows the site of the medieval castle, subseqently covered by a jumble of property including the cone of an early steel cementation furnace.

The lower end of the Fitzalan Market Hall or Shambles, in Haymarket, c.1905. It had been redesigned for the Duke of Norfolk in 1856 with the Exchange News Rooms and Telegraph office on the upper floor. Statues of Mercury and Vulcan in niches flank the windows. Demolition of the Hall in 1930 ended some seven hundred years of market trading on that spot.

The Yellow Lion, Haymarket, shortly before it was demolished for a Woolworth's in 1928. Its heyday was the early Victorian era, when many friendly societies met in its rooms. It was a centre for country coaches and carriers and there was a Friday market in the yard for calves and lambs.

The Brightside and Carbrook Co-operative Society's City Stores on Exchange Street, 1930. The arcade also gave access to the Castle Market, which replaced the Fitzalan Market Hall. The chauffeur-driven Rolls appears to indicate a high class of customer.

The Chinese tea rooms in the Brightside and Carbrook Co-op's enlarged City Stores, 1930. A choice of four restaurants was provided. The old established department stores were wooing customers with lounges, club rooms and smoke rooms, and the Co-op was meeting the competion head on.

The Old Killing Shambles on the site of the Castle shortly before demolition in 1928. They had been moved here from the bottom of High Street in the eighteenth century, but remained a dubious amenity in the City Centre. Cattle had to be driven along the streets from the railway sidings, with the occasional stampede occurring en route.

Cattle arriving at the Killing Shambles. The new Corporation abattoir opened on Cricket Inn Road in 1929 and was served by its own railway sidings.

Three
The Ponds

The River Sheaf gave its name to Sheffield and formed the southern defences of the Castle. It is now largely underground. The River Porter joins the Sheaf under the north end of platform five of the railway station. In the Middle Ages both rivers fed a series of ponds, which over the years were extended and adapted to a variety of industrial purposes. By the nineteenth century they had become general rubbish tips. After every thunderstorm they were swelled by the flushings of the yards and alleys of Park Hill. Flooding was also a problem; the old Shrewsbury Hospital was by the river and some pensioners were drowned in 1811. The construction of the Midland Railway and Sheaf Street in the 1860s culverted most of the river and was regarded as a great improvement. Across the Sheaf from the Castle were the Castle Orchards. This relatively flat land was chosen for the Canal Basin when the Sheffield Canal extended into the town in 1819. Nearby, in place of his Hospital, the Duke of Norfolk built his Corn Exchange and replaced it with a grander version in 1881. Sheffield Hallam University, Ponds Forge, Sheaf Roundabout and the Transport Interchange have now transformed the area.

Sheaf Street looking up Exchange Street c.1935, showing the lower end of Norfolk Market Hall. Horse drawn vehicles are assembling in front of the Castlefolds Fruit and Vegetable Market, which was replaced by the present Sheaf Market in 1973. The Setts Market occupies the space where the carts are waiting.

Lucy, John and Jane Donnelly and an assistant in front of their stall at Castlefolds Fruit Market, c.1902.

The imposing Corn Exchange built for the Duke of Norfolk in 1881. The view is looking north along Sheaf Street c.1910, with the New Market Hotel on the right. Broad Street branches off between the two buildings. The central hall of the Corn Exchange was gutted by fire in 1947 and the offices surrounding it were demolished in 1964.

Pedestrians dodging traffic on the Belisha crossing on Sheaf Street, c.1948, a view taken from the Corn Exchange windows in the opposite direction to the photograph above. Sheaf Market is seen across the street with Commercial Street beyond. Horse transport is now in decline. The traffic includes two railway lorries based at the numerous goods yards in the area.

Baker's Hill, c.1900, looking across the Sheaf valley to Park Hill. Now reduced to a flight of steps by the side of the Post Office, Baker's Hill was once the main vehicular road which linked Norfolk Street with Shude Hill and the Duke of Norfolk's bridge over the Sheaf into the Park. The buildings on the left include an eighteenth-century town house, inelegantly sub-divided. Note the wooden rainwater hoppers.

Shude Hill at the foot of Baker's Hill, c.1900. Commercial Street, constructed by the Midland Railway as part of the price for cutting through the Ponds in 1870, crosses on a standard Midland Railway bridge. The magnificent offices of the Sheffield United Gaslight Company, built in 1875, made use of both levels.

Pond Street, 1937. Many rural bus services started after the First World War, and established Pond Street as their City terminus. After 1930 independent operators co-existed fairly peacefully with the Corporation. Wigmore's bus, in the centre, is about to set off for Dinnington; the double-deckers belong to Sheffield. By 1938 when a site was cleared for a bus station, forty one routes were in operation.

Pond Street Bus Station, c.1950, busy with evening crowds. Many of the inter-war housing estates were poorly served by the trams, whose fate was sealed in 1951. The rudimentary bus station acquired more satisfactory shelters in 1956. East Bank, before the Norfolk Park Flats were built, offers a distant view of the countryside.

The building known today as the Old Queen's Head, Pond Hill, 1862. It has gone through many vicissitudes. When built c.1500 it was evidently a place of some consequence attached to the Shrewsburys' estate, perhaps as a banqueting hall for parties hunting or shooting wildfowl on the Earl's ponds. Illustrations made soon after 1800 show that it was already the object of antiquarian interest, apparently in residential use and well cared for. About 1840 James Pilley, a rivet maker, opened a beer house next door (to the left of the picture) which he called the Old Queen's Head. In 1862 the fortunes of the old building were at a low ebb, and it was occupied by George Mower who let out horses and carriages. It has of course since been merged into the pub and undergone many restorations.

Pond Street c.1895, showing nos 193-7, where Sheaf House now stands. Gebhardt's was a branch establishment; Ferdinand Gebhardt came from Germany c.1880 and opened a shop on the Moor making "pork pies and the celebrated tomato sausages". The Moor establishment narrowly escaped the fury of a patriotic mob in 1915, though German pork butchers had been settled in Sheffield for at least a hundred years.

The Midland Station, originally known as Pond Street, c.1908. All the frontage seen here was a new extension, completed in time for the Royal Visit in 1905. Park Hill provides the skyline, with St Luke's Church and the chimney of Greaves' Norfolk Brewery.

Midland Station c.1910 from platform two, showing the railway side of the new extension. The original station of 1870 is to the left; a few years previously horse cabs would have drawn up where the short train for the north is seen awaiting departure. The bookstall beneath the footbridge has only recently been removed.

Departure of the City Battalion from the Midland Station, 13 May 1915. The Battalion was made up of volunteers from the University and "professional classes" in the City and was given a civic send-off. In fact they were only going as far as Cannock Chase and it would be six months before they were sent abroad and a year before they were on the Front and preparing for the Battle of the Somme. Colonel Mainwaring and officers are facing the men; the Chief Constable's Civilian Corps are drawn up behind to keep girl friends and sisters at bay.

The entrance to the Sheaf Market, popularly known as the "Rag and Tag", at the corner of Commercial Street and Sheaf Street, c.1937, with a pictorial illuminated display by Novel Signs. The Corporation left the open "Rag and Tag" much as it was when they took it over from the Duke of Norfolk in 1899. Its replacement by the new indoor market in 1973 was not warmly received.

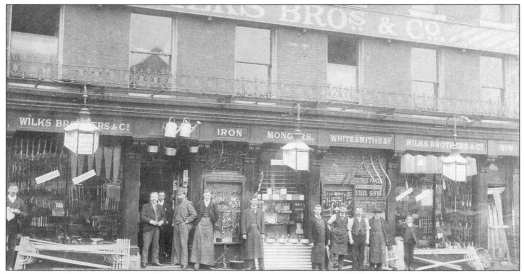

Wilks Bros' ironmonger's shop, 9 Furnival Street, 1892. John Wilks set up business as a cutler in 1744. In 1833 his descendent Joseph moved to Furnival Street where he made brass, steel and wrought iron grates and palisades for tombs. By 1892 the range of wares had widened, though a fine decorative palisade will be noted. They remained a family business until 1956, and finally closed on Mulberry Street in 1972.

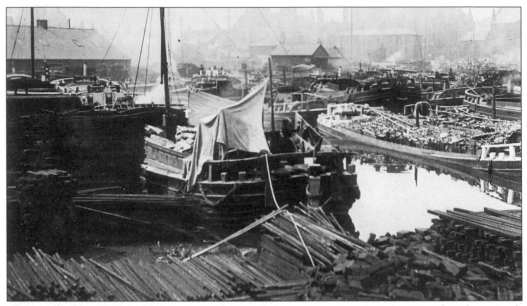

The south side of the Canal Basin, 1887. With its companion view opposite the photograph was taken when resentment at railway control of canals was widespread and ship canals were under discussion. The pictures show that neither low water nor railway management was preventing goods from reaching Sheffield. Iron bar, timber and coal are in evidence, but handling and storage facilities were woefully inadequate. Note the sail drying, and the captain's wife hanging out the washing.

The Alexandra Theatre (alternatively Opera House, Old Alex, Tommy's or Blood Tub), Blonk Street, c.1910. It stood opposite the drive to Victoria Station. "Tommy" was Thomas Youdan, who moved there after the loss of his Surrey Theatre by fire in 1864, and developed it into a rival of the Theatre Royal. The annual outing to the Alexandra (which he offered free) was the only theatrical experience allowed the inmates of the Sheffield Workhouse. Under a previous incarnation as the Adelphi, it had claimed to be the only stage in Sheffield capable of accommodating an elephant, a boast put to the test in their 1856 pantomime *Bluebeard, or female curiosity*.

The north side of the Canal Basin, 1887. Conditions were particularly cramped on this side as the MS&LR, who bought the canal in 1848, used part of the wharf to construct their coal depot, seen on the arches on the right. This left the canal with the original terminal warehouse of 1819, seen in the background, to which the railway added a grain warehouse at right angles. In the event Sheffield never got its ship canal, though there was some investment in the Basin in the 1890s. The most spectacular legacy of this is the steel and concrete warehouse which now straddles the basin and blocks the view seen here.

The backstage of the Alexandra was built on girders over the River Sheaf, here seen from Exchange Street Bridge in 1913. The Alex was demolished in in 1914 to make Castlegate and the Sheaf was culverted.

Victoria Station at midday on 16 August 1875. The normally gloomy train shed found itself transformed into a giant conservatory and the carpet was out to receive the Prince and Princess of Wales on their way to open Firth Park. They were not actually due to arrive until 2.30 when their train would be heralded by a volley of canon from the top of Park Hill. The shining and beflagged locomotive is probably MS&LR no 153, about to set out for Retford to meet the Special. Victoria Station had been opened in 1851 and the Hotel ten years later. From this day the Hotel was to be known as the Royal Victoria. There was much talk at the end of the century of having a combined Central Station to replace the two unsatisfactory ones, but the railway companies showed no enthusiasm. Improvements to the Midland Station spurred the Great Central to extend Victoria in 1908. Despite the electrification of its principal service to Manchester, Victoria was closed in 1971 and, apart from the hotel, few traces now remain.

Four
Norfolk Street, Fitzalan Square

Norfolk Street was an eighteenth century creation. Its north side touched the back gardens of houses on High Street, a favourite location for Dissenters to build chapels. The Duke himself followed the trend with a Catholic chapel at the back of his own house (now St Marie's). In 1720, at the top of the street and at the extreme edge of the town, they built the Baroque Anglican Church of St Paul. The south side of Norfolk Street was now ripe for development and a geometrical grid of streets was laid out by the Duke's steward, who named most of them after his master, but one, Eyre Street, after himself. One or two eighteenth-century houses remain, but the area is better remembered for its cutlery works, its theatres and the cultural delights of Surrey Street. Arundel Gate has since upset Vincent Eyre's orderly grid pattern and has cut Norfolk Street off from Fitzalan Square. This much needed open space was created after 1875 by clearing the buildings between Market Street (once the slaughter houses), Jehu Lane and Baker's Hill. As the photographs demonstrate, it was a long time before the square was fronted by buildings of any architectural distinction.

Fitzalan Square c.1890, a view looking down Commercial Street and contriving to catch three reasonably stately Victorian buildings in one group. The clear sky still showing down Commercial Street betrays the slow and uncertain pace of nineteenth-century redevelopment. On the corner of Haymarket, extreme left, was the Post Office, in the building which it had occupied since 1871, though sorting took place in Pond Street. The magnificent premises on Commercial Street were the offices of the Sheffield United Gaslight Company. In spite of the best efforts of the Corporation, this was the one public utility which was never run by the City. On the right is a recently arrived invader, the Birmingham, Dudley and District Banking Company, later District, and eventually Barclays' Bank. Though handsome in detail, it was criticized for its top heavy and unbalanced appearance. In 1969 it was pulled down, and a new bank built behind.

Fitzalan Square from the bottom of Norfolk Street, c.1905. The tram is literally at the end of the line. The Bell Hotel and the 1871 Post Office building are still recognizable. Wonderland was an entertainment booth which occasionally showed early cinema films; it was later the site for the Electra Palace. The building with the clock tower is the cab stand, or Idle Man's Rest.

Fitzalan Square after remodelling in 1913 to accommodate the statue of King Edward VII which, surprisingly, has yet to be moved. The Post Office, completed in 1910, provides a familiar background. The exotic Electra Palace on the left was opened in 1911 and survived, with most of its charms well concealed, as the Classic Cinema until burnt out in 1984.

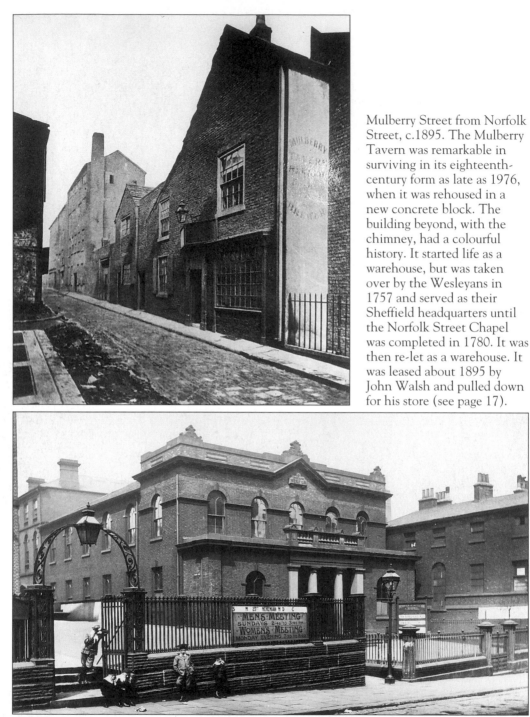

Mulberry Street from Norfolk Street, c.1895. The Mulberry Tavern was remarkable in surviving in its eighteenth-century form as late as 1976, when it was rehoused in a new concrete block. The building beyond, with the chimney, had a colourful history. It started life as a warehouse, but was taken over by the Wesleyans in 1757 and served as their Sheffield headquarters until the Norfolk Street Chapel was completed in 1780. It was then re-let as a warehouse. It was leased about 1895 by John Walsh and pulled down for his store (see page 17).

The Wesleyan Chapel, Norfolk Street, c.1905. Norfolk Street is still noted for its chapels. By 1800 Unitarians, Roman Catholics, Congregationalists and Wesleyans were accommodated. The Nether Chapel (Congregational) is through the gateway on the left. The lamp post marks the entrance to Chapel Walk. In 1906 the Wesleyan Chapel was pulled down for the Victoria Mission.

Miss Jessop laying the foundation stone of the Channing Hall in New Surrey Street, 14 June 1881, on behalf of her father, the steelmaster of Brightside Forge. The Unitarian Upper Chapel, to which the Hall is connected, can be seen behind. In relation to their numbers, Upper Chapel members were extraordinarily prominent in Sheffield public life, providing numerous Mayors, Master Cutlers and magistrates.

The wedding of George Arthur Stables, clerk, to Amy Swift at Nether Congregational Chapel,14 June 1920. Bride and groom lived in the suburbs but were married in the City Centre. The tall man in the back row is Mr Reuben Tyas Hague, a manager, and cousin of the bride. They both lived in Woodseats.

The former Assembly Rooms in Norfolk Street, c.1893, waiting for a new occupant. It was built in 1762 back-to-back with the Theatre, a leisure centre for the new money of eighteenth-century Sheffield. Later, outclassed by the Music Hall, it was used as a Council Chamber from 1847 to 1868, when the councillors found they could save money by moving into the Free Library. It was demolished following the Theatre Royal fire in 1936.

Sheffield's Theatreland, c.1910. This view shows Tudor Street, looking across Arundel Street in the distance. The Theatre Royal, direct successor to the Theatre of 1763, is on the left. Facing it is the Lyceum, an extravagant refurbishment, inside and out, of the City Theatre of 1890. This itself was a replacement of a wooden circus where the Leno family once performed. The new Lyceum, designed to out-dazzle the Empire, opened in 1897. Much of the external plasterwork was subsequently lost or obscured – it is said the urns were removed in the War to prevent their crushing someone in an air raid – and its recent restoration is an example of what can be done to retain the best of what remains of Victorian Sheffield.

Opposite: Tudor Street, c.1930. The much rebuilt Theatre Royal is at the end of the row. The building between the Theatre and John Round's Tudor Spoon and Fork Works had been the Royal Pavilion Music Hall before most of Sheffeld's smaller halls succumbed to competition from the Empire Palace and the strictures of fire inspectors.

Hoses playing across Arundel Street from the roof of the Adelphi Hotel as the Theatre Royal burns, 30 December 1935. By this time it was operating under the same management as the Lyceum, where straight drama was concentrated. As there were no casualties, in the economic climate they probably regarded it little more than a sentimental loss and the ruins were soon reduced to a car park.

The comic team from the Theatre Royal pantomime *Jack and Jill* which opened on Christmas Eve, 1925. Here are Mr Jack Stanley as Archibald Smiler and Mr Johnnie Schofield as Martha Crump. The *Sheffield Telegraph* critic found they "kept the laughter freely going whenever they were in the scene", and as for Mr Ivor White as Simple Simon (front row), he "simply stole the show".

Advertising placard for the Lyceum pantomime, 1907.

The Medical School, corner of Arundel Street and Surrey Street, for sale in 1888. The School had moved to Leopold Street. There had been a discreet trade in unmarked boxes from the Workhouse to the Dissecting Room and out again to Wardsend Cemetery. It was latterly an army recruiting office. On demolition, the Latin inscription, which had faithfully served both occupants, was removed to Beechill Road.

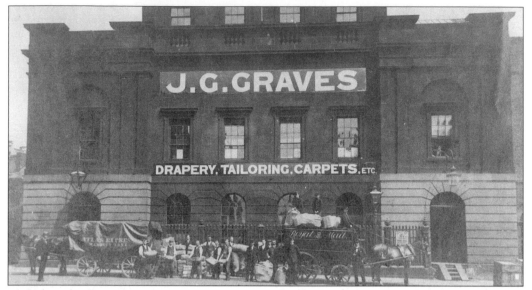

The Music Hall on Surrey Street, in use as a warehouse by J.G. Graves, c.1902. Goods which have been ordered from his catalogues are seen being dispatched by mail; Graves enjoyed a stormy relationship with the GPO, of whom he was a very large customer. The Music Hall opened in 1824 as a concert hall. In 1908 it became the Lending Department of the Central Library.

The first of a new Central Library building, which was to replace the former Mechanics' Institute, nears completion on Surrey Street, 1932. Library operations continued in the dilapidated ex-Music Hall down the street. This scheme at the depths of the Depression provided some work for building trades, but would not have gone ahead without a large gift from J.G. Graves.

Opening the Graves art gallery on the top floor of the Central Library Building, 5 July 1934. The Duchess of York, dressed in palest blue silk, admires exhibits onder the guidance of Dr Rothenstein, the Director. The inclusion of the Art Gallery in the building was an afterthought; it clinched the Graves gift and enabled the whole project to go ahead.

Library staff on the roof of the Central Library building line up for fire-watching duties in 1940, with tin hats, lamps and stirrup pumps at the ready. Mary Walton, Reference Librarian and local historian, is on the back row, extreme right.

Mr Douglas Marshall and his staff outside his Empire Trading Stamp shop, 19-23 Howard Street, Christmas 1921. He was selling tea on St Philip's Road in 1889, and subsequently branched out into china and earthenware. The Empire Trading Stamp Company was developed after the First World War.

The Drapery Department at the Empire Trading Stamp shop, c.1935.

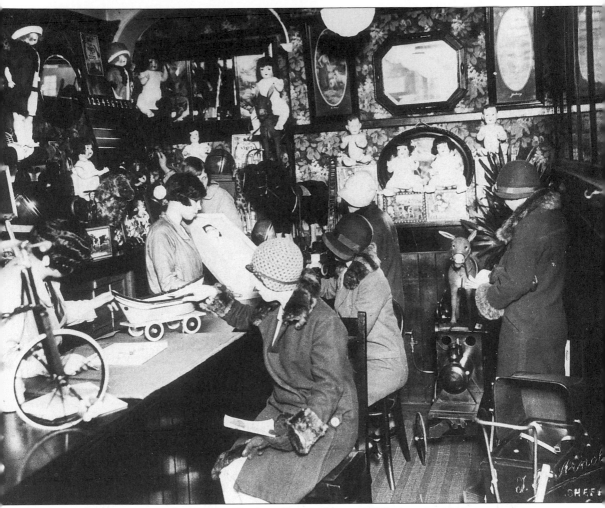

The Toy Department at the Empire Trading Stamp shop, c.1935. A series of photographs was taken at this time. A relatively small establishment is emulating the style of the great City stores under slightly cramped circumstances. Some doubling up of staff was necessary. "Customers" appear to be inspecting goods which they have selected from a catalogue. The business closed before the Second World War. There had been a branch establishment at New Mills, where Mr Marshall also owned a cinema.

Looking south-east from the Town Hall tower, c.1907. The Victoria Mission Hall on Norfolk Street is complete up to the tower and work is, as always, in progress improving the Post Office. The roofs of the Theatre Royal dominate the right middle distance, with Hays' Wine Vaults (now the Ruskin Museum) providing a convenient point of modern reference in front of them. Towards the skyline, Broad Street can be seen leading up to St John's Church, Park Hill. The large, low building at the foot of Broad Street was the LNWR goods station and its stumpy tower was the reservoir for the hydraulic lifts which gave access to the high level railway tracks.

Five

Town Hall

Sheffield had a town hall long before it had a town council. In the eighteenth century there was a little building in a corner of the Churchyard which was replaced in 1808 by a larger one on the corner of Castle Street and Waingate. This has gradually expanded into the present County Court building. Both halls belonged to the Town Trustees, a body which traces its origin to the Charter granted by Lord Furnival to the free burgesses of Sheffield in 1297. When the Town Council was first elected in 1843 they had to hire somewhere to meet. It was not until 1886 that they decided after heated debate to purchase a site next to St Paul's Church and invite architects to submit suitable plans. In 1890 the design of the London architect E.W. Mountford was accepted against local competition; embellishments continued to arouse fierce opposition on grounds of extravagance. Eventually a lot of money proved well spent on a dignified building which Queen Victoria was able to open on 21 May 1897 by remote control without descending from her carriage in Pinstone Street. On the St Paul's side it was not completed until 1923. In 1977 a separate building in aggressively modern style was completed across Norfolk Street. Popularly known as the Egg Box, it contrasts with the soaring towers and sweeping gables of Mountford's "old" Town Hall.

A view of the corner of Fargate and Pinstone Sreet c.1890, showing property which was demolished to make way for the new Town Hall. The professional classes who lived next to St Paul's in the eighteenth century had long moved away. A typical cutlers' works is seen on New Church Street.

New Church Street looking towards Pinstone Street, c.1890. It was cleared for the new Town Hall in 1891. The view includes the Green Man pub and one of the several Cutlers' Arms among other traces of a more elegant Georgian past.

Reuben Thompson's four-in-hand coach sets off on a day trip to the Peak District from New Surrey Street, c.1890. On sunny days the Victorians were apt to feel nostalgic for Georgian stage coaches, rather as we do for their steam railways, and the "Old Times" coaches were popular in summer. A typical route was by Fox House and Hathersage to Calver Sough and back up Froggat Edge. The pace downhill could be quite exciting. New Surrey Street was extended from old Surrey Street across Norfolk Street to Fargate in 1881, carving through much eighteenth-century property including the Assay Office (see page 23). The Town Hall will fill the left hand of the picture, while the right hand side of the new street has been completed as far as the new Channing Hall.

The City Council at its first meeting in the new oak-panelled Council Chamber on Pinstone Street, 2 June 1897. The Duke of Norfolk, last Mayor, first Lord Mayor (and by coincidence Lord of the Manor), presides, flanked by the Aldermen and overlooking Mr Bramley, the Town Clerk. In the body of the hall the Father of the Council, Joe Nadin the herbalist (fifth from the left, back row) had represented St Philip's Ward since 1858. A newcomer, to his right on the row below, is Councillor J.G. Graves who was to finance many benefactions to the City out of the proceeds of his successful mail order business. Some of the members were still not entirely reconciled to the cost of such a lavish new building, but there were obvious advantages in having most of the departmental offices under one roof.

Opposite: Another tea party, this time on the Town Hall steps, December, 1940. Town Hall workers and members of the Home Guard take refreshment from one of the Church Army mobile canteens during the week of the Blitz. One of the canteens was in Church Street on the night of the 11th and was a total loss.

A tea party at the Town Hall, with the Lady Mayoress, Miss Mary Longden, presiding, 19 July 1937. Ald. Mrs Longden was the first woman Lord Mayor of Sheffield, and it was her daughter's idea to invite the 17 boys and 10 girls born on Coronation Day, together with their mothers. It was a piece of soft advertising for the Child Welfare Clinic, who were at hand to offer advice and refreshment. Miss Calladine was also engaged on the piano to play soothing music.

Pinstone Street from the Town Hall clock tower, c.1909. There is a good view of the top of St Paul's tower (an afterthought – it originally finished below the clock) and the Prudential Building, which is now Laura Ashley. Away beyond St Paul's is the tower of St Mary's Bramall Lane and the two church towers at Highfield. Just to the right of the centre is the tower of Berry's Moorhead Brewery.

Town Hall Square, c.1895 looking up Barker's Pool. The obelisk commemorated Queen Victoria's Jubilee of 1887 but never proved very popular and was moved to Endcliffe Park in 1903. The shop on the right, familiar to several generations as Wilson Peck's Beethoven House, was built in 1884 for Johnson and Appleyard, the cabinet makers. They claimed to enjoy Royal Appointment and incorporated the Royal Arms on the front of their building, where it can still be seen.

Town Hall Square just before the First World War. Queen Victoria has supplanted the obelisk, Wilson Peck's have moved into Beethoven House, and Sheffield has just acquired a magnificent, gleaming white Cinema House. Behind the Cinema House can be glimpsed the upper windows of the Grand Hotel.

Queen Victoria, dismounted from her pedestal and roped on a lorry, on her way to join the obelisk in Endcliffe Park, 24 February 1930. This was a controversial move. Her statue, commissioned from Alfred Turner and unveiled in May 1905 in time for her son's next visit, proved a popular replacement for the old "tooth-pick". Nevertheless the traffic engineers prevailed.

Town Hall Square from the Lord Mayor's balcony, looking up Leopold Street, 1943. There is little evidence of a war being on except for the blackout screens covering shop windows and the black and white bases of the Belisha beacons to enable them to be distinguished in the dark. After Queen Victoria departed there were some short-lived and visually unhappy experiments in traffic control before the rock garden was established, just in time, it is said, for some of the smaller rocks to come in useful as missiles against the Town Hall windows during the unemployment demonstrations of the thirties. Orchard Square now dominates the centre of the scene. From this point it is evident that the Victorian shop fronts preserved on Leopold Street are out of line with it; in fact they follow the line of the eighteenth-century Brelsforth Orchards, swept away by the Victorian improvers.

Six

Moorhead

Below Cambridge Street the town is subtly different. Newcomers are surprised to to find yet another shopping centre extending down the Moor, and students of Debrett may notice the Norfolk family and estate names which streets and pubs have hitherto displayed give way to Rockinghams, Miltons and Fitzwilliams. We have crossed into the Manor and Township of Ecclesall. The Moor was Ecclesall's moor until it was enclosed in 1789 and Earl Fitzwilliam set up his own rival market place, known as the Ecclesall Bazaar. It was not successful, but the Moor (officially South Street, Moor) became a busy shopping street. The Crimean War was a very popular cause in Sheffield. A monument was commissioned but enthusiasm was not matched by money and it was seven years before it was complete. The foundation stone was laid by the Duke of Cambridge, and the opportunity was taken to rename Coalpit Lane Cambridge Street. This street had long been the main road from Fargate to the south, and it remained the boundary between Sheffield and Ecclesall. As late as 1930, if you lived on the west side, you had the advantage of paying much lower rates and, when poverty and old age struck, you went to Nether Edge instead of Fir Vale. Pinstone Street was cut through to Moorhead under the 1875 Improvement Act, saving traffic the detour round Barker's Pool and Cambridge Street.

An arch across Pinstone Street about to welcome Queen Victoria, 1897. It was apparently a co-operative effort between two firms of plasterers and decorators, each taking one side. The advertising placards were removed before Her Majesty arrived.

Pinstone Street c.1910, with the Salvation Army Citadel, Town Hall and St Paul's Church. Having purchased its corner site, the Salvation Army prudently developed shops along Pinstone Street which subsidized the Citadel and Hostel behind. Describing the opening in January 1894, the *War Cry* was pleased to find the Hall "attractive and not yet too respectable".

Pinstone Street, 1909 – not the chaos when the trams first came to Pinstone Street but the renewed chaos ten years later when the worn-out rails needed to be replaced. At least the trams themselves kept going with the help of temporary tracks by-passing the new works. Wear on the rails was a constant problem, especially on points and crossings, though Hadfields' New Era manganese steel worked wonders. The Sheffield Tramways system provided a handy demonstration for home and overseas customers. The passing loop and familiar wooden shelters on St Paul's side of Pinstone Street were installed in 1933.

Surplus land from the Corporation's Pinstone Street improvement scheme up for sale, c.1890. The buyer was to be the Salvation Army. Cross Burgess Street is on the left and the tower looming in the background belongs to the Albert Hall (see page 86).

Thomas and Taylor's outfitters and Army Stores, 37-41 Cambridge Street, c.1934. Mr W.J. Taylor, the proprietor, stands in the top doorway with his daughter. Hiking, rambling and camping in the Peak District became a local cult during the Depression; it was healthy and above all cheap. There was a steady demand for robust and serviceable equipment.

The Empire Palace of Varieties on Charles Street, designed by Frank Matcham, opened in 1895 and set a new standard in opulence for Sheffield theatres. There was big money behind it in the Moss Empire's organization in London, who could command the top music hall stars of the day. It was the first Sheffield theatre which had a roof which opened to let the smoke out or, more probably, in. It also staged the first cinematic demonstration in Sheffield in 1896. Battered but unbowed, it survived the Blitz, which destroyed both flanking shops, but succumbed to demolition in 1959.

Union Street from Moorhead c.1911, showing the new Picture Palace on the right. This was Sheffield's first purpose-built cinema, comparatively restrained in style. It was demolished in 1964 in favour of Redvers House. One can speculate whether Sheffield pedestrians ever obeyed the instructions on the lamp post.

Moorhead, with the monument to the Crimean heroes surmounted by the statue of "Queen Victoria as Honour". The guns below were captured at Sebastopol. The photograph was taken about 1890 when this was the terminus for the horse trams to the western suburbs. In the centre is an Eades Patent reversible car which has duly reversed and is about to set off for Nether Edge.

A crowded scene on a showery day at Moorhead, c.1890. Passengers who arrived by tram had to change onto one of the Tramway Company's buses to take them forward to the Town Centre or to the other termini at Lady's Bridge or West Bar.

Crowds watching the procession as Edward VII and Queen Alexandra pass the Crimean Monument, 12 July 1905. The gentlemen with the long beards and many medals are themselves surviving heroes of the Crimean War.

Moorhead, c.1930. The monument has now attracted a jumble of guns, toilets, drinking fountain, telephone booth and an oriental kiosk supplying information on trams and buses. All this was eventually swept away for Furnival Gate. The guns had gone during the war and the top and bottom sections of the monument ended up in the Botanical Gardens.

The Moor (then known as South Street) in 1887, with flags and banners proc- laiming Queen Victoria's Jubilee. The square, striped banner on the left is the contribution of John Atkinson, the draper, whose family store is still a familiar landmark on the Moor. Joseph Puttrell's decorator's shop can also be seen.

The Punch Bowl Hotel on the Moor, c.1890. There was a small market in front, which sold rabbits and pottery. As a pub the Punch Bowl can be traced back to the beginning of the nineteenth century, but it may well be a survivor of the merchants' houses built when the Moor was first enclosed in 1789. It was finally demolished, much altered, in 1938. It stood on the west side, just below the present Fitzwilliam Gate.

The Moor in 1949, showing the devastating effects of the Blitz, which has, incidentally, opened a view of Button Lane on the left, part of a pattern of old streets destroyed by Furnival Gate and Charter Square. On the left skyline is the back of the Hippodrome on Cambridge Street, the largest theatre in Sheffield when it opened in 1907 but since the First World War mostly used as a cinema.

A traveller's porter on the Moor c.1890, when commercial travellers were dependent on the railways and knew Bradshaw's timetable backwards. Porters met them at the railway stations and accompanied them on their rounds, wheeling their samples on a handcart like the one seen here.

These painters and decorators have provided their own title to this photograph, which was taken in their yard off the Moor (see page 80). Apart from Mr J., Mr H. and Mr C. Puttrell, there were 49 staff in 1901. Union rates were £1 9s. 9d. for a 42 hour week, which does not compare too badly with the average earnings of a skilled cutler. They were members of the Amalgamated Society of Painters and Decorators. Mr Joseph Puttrell junior was a distinguished climber and cave explorer and a regular broadcaster between the Wars.

The Brunswick Wesleyan Chapel at the foot of the Moor, c.1905. Ecclesall Road (as it was) branched off in the left foreground. Ellin Street and the Brunswick Vestry Hall are across the road on the extreme left. The Brunswick Chapel of 1834 was regarded as the most elegant of Sheffield's many chapels and when new it competed with the Anglican St Mary's to attract residents of this wealthy surburb. It closed in 1943 when the congregation merged with Trinity Church Highfield. The inner ring road traffic now charges across its site.

Seven

Barker's Pool and Townhead

Barker's Pool and Townhead. Barker's Pool was named from the first artificial water supply to Sheffield, which is thought to have been provided by one "Barker of Balme" and existed in the sixeenth century. It was the highest point of the town and water could be conveniently guided by sluices and channels to most parts. The practice continued in case of fire and for street cleaning until 1793, when the Pool was filled in. By this time the town was extending westwards over Carver Fields and Bailey Fields. The Water Company built a new reservoir nearby which is now somewhere under the N.U.M. Headquarters. Holly Street, once Blind Lane, led along the western edge of the old town to Pinfold Street, where there were some ancient buildings around the Townhead Cross. On the town side of Holly Street were the Brelsforth Orchards, commemorated in Orchard Street and Lane and most recently in Orchard Square. By 1850 they were built over with a typical Sheffield mixture of houses and workshops, including a gas works and at least one steel works. The next fifty years saw a major transformation with the creation of Leopold Street and handsome buildings to go with it, including the Education Offices, Firth College and a new Assay Office. By 1930 the last of the old property had been swept away and the City Hall was taking shape.

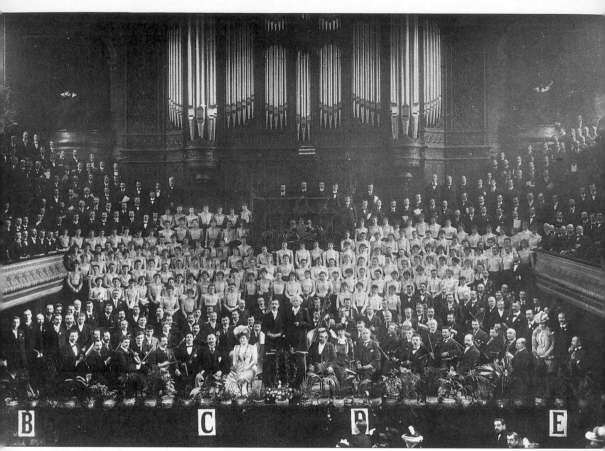

The Albert Hall, Barker's Pool at the conclusion of the second triennial Music Festival, 13 October 1899. August Manns, conducting the augmented Crystal Palace Orchestra shares the honours with Dr Henry Coward, Chorus Master of the Sheffield Festival Chorus. Clara Butt, Elgar and Hubert Parry had also taken part. The Festival Chorus reached the pinnacle of its fame with its Empire tour, "round the world on wings of song", in 1911. The Albert Hall was opened in 1873 and was especially celebrated for its magnificent French organ. After the First World War it became a cinema, and Hall and organ were destroyed by fire in 1937.

The Sheffield War Memorial, Barker's Pool, being unveiled by Lt-Gen Sir Charles Harrington, 28 October 1925. Cambridge Street is on the right. After much controversy, the design of C.D. Carus-Wilson of the University was adopted, but his proposed wooden mast was replaced by one of steel. It had to be manufactured in Hull and its 90ft length caused many problems on its way to Barker's Pool.

A crowded Armistice Day ceremony at the War Memorial, 11 November 1931. Builders completing the City Hall have a good vantage point. The Hall itself had originally been proposed as a memorial to the City's war dead, money having been collected on this understanding. The argument was eventually settled by designating a Memorial Hall at the rear of the main building.

Division Street c.1905, from Barker's Pool. Cambridge Street is on the left, with the "Iron Man" and the Albert Hotel beyond. On the right is Holly Street and the familiar front of the N.U.M. Headquarters, built for the Water Company in 1867. In the distance is a sign over Tulley's photographic studios, part of which can still be seen above the San Remo Restaurant.

Samuel and Jabez Pottinger outside their shop at 91-7 Division Street, probably soon after they moved there in 1905. The Pottinger family was long associated with saddlery, though Jabez later left the business to become a newsagent at Hunter's Bar.

Ancient cottages on Balm Green, glimpsed from Barker's Pool about 1880. When built they must have virtually overlooked the Pool. They were probably built as a single farmhouse in the days when the Town Fields lay immediately beyond Holly Street. Down the yard on the left are the furnaces of the Queen's Steel Works on Holly Street. The City Hall obliterated the whole site in 1929.

Holly Street in 1929, looking towards West Street, with the new Central Telephone Exchange in the distance. The City Hall is starting to take shape on the remains of Balm Green on the right. The buildings on the left accommodated a good selection of little mesters, including bone cutters, ivory handle cutters, fluters, staggers, etchers and German silver buffers.

Leopold Street soon after the opening of the Grand Hotel in 1910. The Hotel provided 300 rooms with telephones, a lounge with an orchestra, a ballroom, and self-contained family flats on each floor, as well as the first American bar in Sheffield. The Education Offices beyond had been the pride of the School Board when they opened on the then new Leopold Street in 1879.

Repairs and testing being carried out on domestic electrical equipment at William Johnson and Co., electrical engineers, 49 Leopold Street, c.1925.

A class at the Central Secondary School, Orchard Lane, c.1900. The headmaster, Mr J.W. Iliffe, is on the left, Mr Jimmy Brown on the right and M. Fah, the French master, is half hidden towards the back. This school was opened in 1880 by the Sheffield School Board as a Central Higher Grade School, part of a grand scheme to enable children to progress from the gutter to the university, funded by the rates and without ever moving more than 100 yards from Leopold Street.

Sands Paviours, shortly before 1890. Sands Paviours ran from Orchard Lane to Bow Street, and provided a handy example of the sort of gutter the School Board had in mind. It stood in the way of the Science Schools which were added to the Central Schools in 1895. The cottages offered the standard accommodation of a kitchen-living room, bedroom, cellar and attic.

The Yorkshire Motor Company's garage on the corner of Pinfold Street and Townhead Street, c.1910. Motorists could order a chassis from a range of manufacturers and have the body work constructed to their specification. This garage was one of the first to be purpose built and incorporated a vehicular lift to all floors. The lift house roof can be seen above the parapet. It is believed that it was originally associated with Messrs Golightly's Dart Motor Company, who were agents for Armstrong Whitworth. By 1912 the garage and the agency belonged to Cravens of Darnall, the famous builders of railway rolling stock. In 1919 Armstrongs purchased the Siddeley-Deasley factory in Coventry and the garage is believed to have closed at that time after the loss of the Armstrong agency. The building later became well-known as Needham's Electrical Engineering, and was pulled down in 1971.

The body shop on the first floor of the Yorkshire Motor Co.'s garage, Townhead Street, c.1912. In the centre is William Swain of Swain and Bradshaw, who served his apprenticeship here.

The Band of Hope Gala Car, strategically posed in front of the tea advertisement on Trippet Lane, 1893. The Temperance Movement fought an uphill fight in Sheffield, but enjoyed support from Liberals on the Town Council, many of whom had strong Chapel connexions. Annual galas were held for many years in the Botanical Gardens, where the bears were especially popular.

A court off Bailey Lane, c.1905. The photographer was standing in the doorway of the living room. The sink was to his left, in front of the window. The stone gulley from the sink waste can be seen leading into the paved yard, joining the gulleys which drained the other sinks, and running off to join the street gutter. Behind the photographer will be a spiral staircase giving access to bedroom and attic above and cellar below. Across the yard and immediately behind the back wall will be dwellings in mirror image. This yard is well swept, though the whitewash ("bugblinding") could do with attention. Photographs of slum courts did not often include people, and animals appear even more rarely. A survey of four-footed inhabitants of a similar area in 1877 found pigs, donkeys, goats, calves and rabbits to say nothing of cats and dogs. Many of these animals lived in the cellars.

Eight

Campo Lane and the Crofts

Campo Lane was a narrow and ancient way along the north (unfashionable) side of the Churchyard. It separated the Vicar's Glebe Lands from the Crofts below. Vicar Wilkinson very profitably developed his land in the 1780s, creating St James' Church and Vicar Lane and raising a storm by encroaching (not for the last time) on the graveyard. The Crofts at the western end of Campo Lane consisted of some very old property including the Grammar School, said to have been built of stone from the demolished Castle. By Victorian times no respectable person would have been seen there after dark, and this area was the subject of early slum clearance. Very different was Paradise Square, a refuge for the new eighteenth-century professional and business classes, though this spot too could become quite lively on market days or in the build-up to an election. At the two northern corners of the Churchyard stood the Girls' and Boys' Charity Schools, the buildings readily identifiable though long devoted to other purposes. At its east end Campo Lane merges into the Hartshead, noted for its long association with the newspaper industry. It is no longer the dark and secluded place it was in the nineteenth century, but there is still a taste of the old town in the narrow streets which lead down from Hartshead to Bank Street and West Bar.

The Parish Church, c.1890. From this angle, apart from the 1960s additions at the west end, virtually the same view could be taken today. This owes much to the extensive restoration and rebuilding in 1880, the extent of which can be judged by the recent pointing. The Churchyard has been reduced by successive widenings of Church Street, a process which provoked popular indignation as early as 1789 and still continues to do so. Railings and gates have gone, but the stone posts can be seen near the east end.

Charity School boys in procession from East Parade past the Church Gates, c.1890. In the eighteenth century they used the Churchyard as a playground, but after objections from the Churchwardens they were confined to playing on the school roof, where railings can still be seen. They moved from East Parade to Brincliffe in 1911.

Celebrations of the centenary of the City Charter in 1943 were somewhat muted because of the war, but there was a pageant in the City Hall and a series of Thanksgiving Services were held at the Cathedral. The Women's Land Army was represented.

Schoolchildren arriving for a special service, 26 August 1943. They had been selected for the strength of their voices and could be heard from passing tramcars.

Looking up Townhead Street to Campo Lane and St James' Church, c.1895. The buildings on the left were part of the Crofts, a notorious area demolished in the first Corporation slum clearance scheme in 1898. In their place the Townhead Street Council Flats were provided, but the rents of 3s. to 6s. a week were beyond the means of the people displaced, and the early tenants were Council workers and others with steady incomes. The gable at the top of the street belonged to the Burns public house, while across the corner of Campo Lane stands the Golden Ball, resited further down Campo Lane by new development in 1968.

Sunday School teachers and scholars in front of St James' Church, with the Vicar, the Rev. Dawson Parsons, the Curate, and Mr Job Preston, Superintendent of the Sunday School until 1922, standing at the rear. St James' was constructed as an overspill for the Parish Church in 1789. It was declared redundant in 1936 and had closed before fire bombs gutted the building in 1940.

The Golden Ball at the corner of Townhead Street and Campo Lane, c.1937. A rare glimpse inside a Sheffield pub. Mr T.W. Brookes, on the right, was the landlord and Mr Tom Ward the barman. The Golden Ball was popular with actors from the Playhouse across the road.

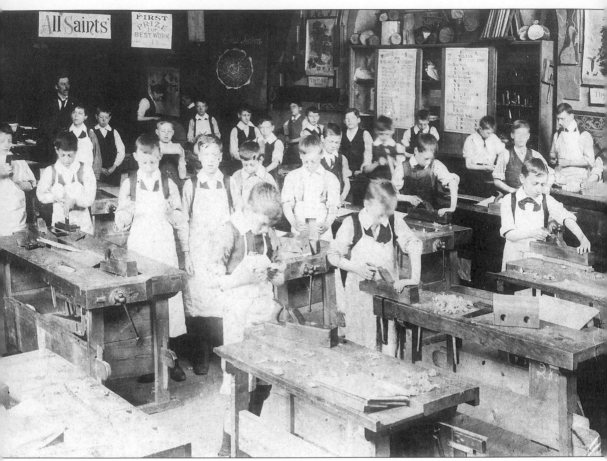

A class from All Saints' School, Ellesmere Road, display their prize-winning woodworking skills in the Church House Institute, St James' Street, c.1905. This building (now the Gladstone Pub) opened in 1860 as an Anglican adult education college. After 1903 it hired out rooms to the Education Committee and boys from selected Council schools came in for woodwork lessons by tram.

A mass political meeting in Paradise Square, seen from the balcony of the Middle Class School. This scene confronted all who aspired to represent Sheffield in Parliament. Some candidates never got past this stage. John Heiffor's windows overlooked twenty-five years of electioneering, seeing Sheffield swing from Liberal to Conservative. The date is probably some time in the 1890s. There are no signs of the supplies of free beer, activities of hired thugs and hecklers climbing up the lamp post which characterized earlier meetings.

Paradise Square at a quieter period, c.1895. Solicitors and surveyors have already taken over the east side, but the north side could boast a private school, a printing office and Mrs Eliza and Miss Lydia Fisher's glass and china shop. A visit to the Square will reveal that it looks more Georgian now than it did in 1895.

The Montgomery Tavern, Hartshead in 1862. In the eighteenth century this shop had the largest display windows in town. In 1787 it became Joseph Gales' stationery shop and the printing office of his radical *Sheffield Register*. After Gales had to flee to America in 1794, James Montgomery continued to print the paper, now renamed the *Iris*, while composing hymns and poetry in a back room. His literary activities enjoyed an international reputation. In Sheffield he was involved in almost every charitable and cultural activity. After his retirement to Broomhill the premises became a beerhouse, and by 1862 it was offering meals and beds to carters. The shop front was removed in 1868, parts finding their way to America as souvenirs of Gales.

At the back of the *Sheffield Telegraph* offices, Hartshead, just before the First World War. The plaque on the left indicates the site of the *Iris* printing office, seen on the page opposite. Vans wait to rush the evening *Yorkshire Telegraph and Star* to suburban newsagents. The "Sports Special" is delivered by motorcycle combination. Paper supplies were delivered by cart from Peter Dixon's of Oughtibridge to the store at the end of the block.

Miss Lucas and teddy bear collecting for the boys serving abroad, 1915. She is standing outside her father's offices at 8 East Parade. Mr Lucas was agent for British Thompson Houston, and had been negotiating with the Council over the sale of motor buses.

"Hand composition – old style", a view taken to celebrate fifty years of the *Sheffield Daily Telegraph*, 1905. The composing room was in the top floor of the extensions carried out in 1890 between High Street and Hartshead. The more modern linotype machines can be seen through the arch in the back wall and in fact were responsible for most of the 1,510,103 words in the average Saturday edition. Hand compositors came into their own for display advertising. A pneumatic tube connected the composing room with the office, and advertisers could be supplied with their proofs within minutes. Electric lighting, heating and power for the presses were all supplied by a coke-fired steam engine on the premises.

The counting house at the *Sheffield Telegraph*, c.1905. It appears to be an exclusively male preserve but women were to be found elsewhere in the building. The General Manager's Secretary was one, and the Women's Page had a Lady Editor.

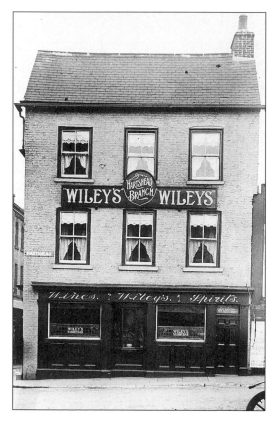

The Dove and Rainbow on Hartshead, c.1930. William Howitt, wandering in search of homes and haunts of the English poets, was upset to find that Hartshead had declined into a "strange hidden court of low eating houses and the dens of pettyfogging lawyers". The Dove and Rainbow was an ancient part of this scene. It was burnt down in 1782 and this building was presumably a replacement. Much frequented by the said lawyers and journalists from the *Sheffield Telegraph*, it was demolished to widen Hartshead in 1957 and relocated nearby.

Scargill Croft off Bank Street, c.1905. The street still exists as a steep route down towards West Bar, and the houses which have now gone were certainly there in the early eighteenth century. They were much older than Bank Street, which was driven across Scargill Croft in 1792.

New Street seen from Bank Street, with Scargill Croft in the background, c.1905. New Street was a continuation downhill of Figtree Lane and was certainly established by 1736. The buildings are probably later eighteenth-century replacements; the shop on the right has typical Sheffield proportions.

Nine

The Wicker and Bridgehouses

The River Don was essential to Sheffields's medieval defences and to its later industrial development, but by Victorian times it was closely hemmed in on both banks by buildings. In the town centre the river was easily visible only from Blonk Street Bridge, Lady's Bridge or Nursery Street. Once across the river you were in the township of Brightside, but still very much in the Manor of Sheffield. Lady's Bridge, built in 1497 and still going strong, led to the Wicker, an open space overlooked from across the river by the Castle. Here the Earl of Shrewsbury's tenants assembled annually with arms and horses and his courts were held. Northwards lay the Spital Fields, named from the pre-Reformation Hospital of St Leonard. In the eighteenth century they served as Ducal nursery gardens (hence Nursery Street) and this postponed building development until the 1790s. Bridgehouses, by contrast, was an ancient settlement and an important road junction; Pye Bank (now Pitsmoor Road) was the old road to the north, much dreaded for its steep gradients. There was a wooden bridge here, later replaced in iron. The railway from Manchester selected Bridgehouses as its terminus in 1845 and after its continuation across the Wicker developed extensive goods yards.

A smoky view up the Don from Lady's Bridge before the First World War. Smoke meant work, and after the war people would have been happy to see more of it. On the left Tennants' Brewery still stands, but without its chimneys. The Millsands Steelworks beyond and Cockers' Wireworks across the river in Nursery Street have long gone.

Looking downstream from Lady's Bridge, with Blonk Street Bridge in the near distance, c.1890. Changes were about to take place on the left which would sweep away the old Huntsman's Forge (with the battlements). Hancock and Lant's premises now occupy most of this site, but the crucible chimney stack at the far end can still be seen from Blonk Street. The fortress-like building beyond is the Tower (or Castle) grinding wheel, which originally rented out premises and steam power to individual little mesters.

The view from Victoria Station approach, looking across a deserted Cattle Market towards Blonk Street, c.1920. The River Don is hidden by the hoardings. Travellers arriving in Sheffield were left in no doubt as to how the City earned its money. Amid a fine display of industrial chimneys, the battlemented ones on the corner of the Tower Wheel were possibly unique in Sheffield.

The Sheffield Fair on the Cattle Market, taken from Victoria Station approach before the First World War. The Fair was a very old Sheffield institution, going back before 1297. Latterly it was held at Whitsun and November. Across the hidden river is the Dannemora Works of Seebohm and Dieckstahl, later Arthur Balfour, which abutted Osborn's Clyde Works.

The Wicker in 1898. The Clyde Works office block, built for Shortridge, Howell and inherited by Samuel Osborn, stands proud on the right. The Corporation had taken over running the trams to Attercliffe and Brightside, but were still using horses. A car has just moved out of the single line terminus to make way for an arrival.

The Wicker shortly before the First World War, with a glimpse up Spital Hill. Trams started running to the Norfolk Arms on Handsworth Road in 1909, through what was then rural West Riding. The Arches, most noble monument in Sheffield to the railway age, are seen coated with grime and plastered with advertisements. The Wicker was the busiest thoroughfare in Sheffield, with four tram routes and heavy traffic from the East End works and to and from the railway goods yards. Owing to its origins as an open space for archery and feudal assemblies, it has never required widening.

Opposite: City Engineer's workers with road resurfacing equipment on Twelve O'Clock Street, between Saville Street and Attercliffe Road, 1926. The Council spent nearly a million pounds in that year on relief work, and 45per cent of it was paid as wages to men who would otherwise have been on the dole. The ones wearing ties were probably office workers.

Donkey and cart at T.W. Ward's scrapyard, The Wicker, May 1937. Tommy Ward bought scrap in all shapes and sizes, from battleships (of which he once possessed a sizeable fleet) to old domestic iron. Here is the humbler end of his supply chain.

The other end of the scale at T.W. Ward's Albion Works, Saville Street. Lizzie the elephant is here seen with her handler and a load of castings. She was requisitioned from a Circus and became a familiar sight in the streets of Sheffield during the First World War.

Fitzalan Street seen from Railway Street, c.1910. This street, now entirely lost, originally extended up the hill from Bridgehouses and was cut off by the railway. The low buildings on the right were occupied by a tripe seller and a fishmonger. One of them is receiving a delivery of barrels from a cart correctly parked against the curb and facing up the gradient.

Mrs Anne Oxspring's butcher's shop, 49 Pye Bank, in 1893, canopy raised to display the meat to best effect. These cuts probably came from the Killing Shambles (page 38) but American and Argentine beef was now available, thanks to advances in refrigeration.

Harvest Lane, looking towards town, c.1920. This part of the lane is now virtually merged in Mowbray Street. The camera has caught a little drama in front of the Old Harrow. The man on the railings, no doubt after a pint or two, seems to have distressed the small boy, who has gone to fetch his Mem. Mem is having a word; the neighbours gather round.

Mowbray Street from Corporation Street, looking towards Neepsend, c.1920. Corporation Street Baths, rebuilt in 1913, are on the left. This was the main tram route to Owlerton, except on match days. There is a crucible stack in the distance and on the extreme right is one of the Engineer's Department's steam lorries.

Ten

West Bar, Shalesmoor, St Philip's

West Bar takes its name from Sheffield's only recorded town gate. Sheffield had no walls and the gate served the mundane purpose of keeping the animals grazing on the Sherramore (Shalesmoor) from wandering back into the town. By the eighteenth century the town had spread along West Bar Green. Across the gardens to the north west a second series of crofts was established, including Hollis Croft, White Croft, Pea Croft (now Solly Street) and Lambert Croft. There was some industrial development, notably some of the first steel furnaces. Eighteenth-century manufacturers were happy to live next to their works, but by the 1850s most housing in the new Crofts was little improvement on the old Crofts off Townhead Street. The area attracted immigrants, especially from Ireland. St Vincent's Church was established on Solly Street in the hope of maintaining order. Sambourne Square (page 120) was where young Sisters of Charity were sent on their first day to see if they would do. Further out of town, James Dixon of Cornish Place, H.E. Hoole of Green Lane Works and William Ibbotson of Globe Works established large factories. Their employees were the aristocrats of labour, highly-skilled, God-fearing men who supplied the congregations at Ebenezer Chapel and St Philip's Church.

West Bar from the bottom of Snig Hill, c.1890. Demolition of the buildings on the right was about to begin. West Bar was a lively place on a Victorian Saturday night, with pubs in profusion, music halls, street performers, orators, quack doctors and the inevitable pickpockets. The horse trams were not popular and were in constant dispute with carters who demanded the right to offload. After 1900 the Grand Hall of Varieties on Coulston Street was the last music hall open in the area, though the proscenium arch of the Britannia on West Bar Green survived blocked up in a warehouse until a recent fire. J.M. Furness, the chemist on the left, was a member of the Town Council and its first historian.

Superintendent Frost (in office from 1895 until 1915) poses with his men in the West Bar Green Fire Station, which opened in 1900 and is now a museum of the fire service. They seem to be waiting for a horse. The balconies around the yard gave access to flats where firemen and their families lived.

The horses in their stables at West Bar Green. Mr Frost was particularly proud of the automatic swing snap harness he had installed. Charlie, Totley, Vulcan and Prince were trained to step forward as soon as they heard the alarm bell. The Harness fell and snapped shut and they were ready to set off as soon as the crew arrived.

A yard between Hollis Croft and Garden Street, c.1910. Broken window panes, one mended with greased paper, ramshackle brickwork with slapdash whitewash, barefoot children, eye patches; classic features of the Sheffield slum. A child appears to be sitting on the stone basin which has been used to collect rainwater from the roofs in the days when water from taps was reserved for cooking and drinking. Gas seems to have been laid on. The pipe protruding below the lower window leads from the kitchen sink. There was a machine tool shop at the bottom of the yard, a likely source of the grit which was responsible for much eye trouble.

Hollis Croft, c.1910. Through the whitewashed doorway is the yard in the opposite photograph. The exterior view reveals that the building was once a manufacturer's house, now in reduced circumstances and converted to tenements. Thomas Harrison, sawmaker, lived on Hollis Croft up to the early nineteenth century, with his works at the bottom of the yard. He then moved to what is now Weston Park. When he died his daughters subscribed to the Classical memorial which can be seen in the Cathedral, spent their inheritance on religious and educational charities and acted as keepers of Sheffield's Evangelical conscience.

A crowd assembles for the photographer on Smithfield, c.1937. Court no 9 on the left had already been demolished; court no 4 on the right was reached through the arched doorway in the recently pointed building. At the bottom of the street is Allen Street Methodist Sunday School, originally opened in 1816 in connexion with Scotland Street Chapel.

Sambourne Square, between Solly Street and Edward Street, c.1920. Solly Street, at the top of the yard, ran at a much higher level, and the houses displaying a massive five storey wall to Sambourne Square were only three storeys high on the other side. The three storey buildings on the left are of typical Sheffield back-to-back proportions, but there was in fact a works yard behind them where you would expect their opposite numbers to be. The square was developed in the 1790s by Thomas Sambourne, a lawyer and property speculator. Further houses were squeezed in over the next fifty years. The privies on the right were by contrast quite modern. The couple on the left are believed to be Mr and Mrs Yates. Mrs Yates was generally called upon if the midwife was delayed. Note the fender in use as a pen for the little boy, and the canary's cage hanging from the bedroom window. The house at the top of the yard, which appears to be derelict, was rented by the tenants as a body. Bicycles were kept in the living room and pigeons in the bedrooms. Sambourne Square was demolished in 1927.

Sambourne Square, looking down towards Edward Street, showing the new improved privies with moveable ashbins. Like the earlier system of fixed ashpits, they relied largely on gravity, but they saved the nightsoil men the task of digging the pits out and passers-by the trouble of dodging round the heap of muck till the cart came to collect it. Someone still had to brush up afterwards, a duty which probably fell to the latest arrival in the yard.

Scotland Street was a narrow thoroughfare famous in Victorian times for its annual spring Feast when it would be decorated from end to end with boughs and saplings dragged from Walkley Bank, and donkey races and other contests were held. These shops were the subject of a compulsory purchase order in 1919. Scotland Street Chapel, which escaped the order, can just be seen on the left.

Furnace Hill playground, opened in October 1933. Slum clearance provided new open spaces, and some of the vacant sites were used for playgrounds for children who had not been rehoused or had been moved to nearby Council flats. The Council, with help from J.G. Graves, provided swings, roundabouts and solid brick shelters, and the permanent supervision of a uniformed Parkie. Sturdy iron railings could be used to exclude wrongdoers. These organized activities replaced traditional improvised games in yards and backstreets, though the state of the vacant property in the background suggests the principal alternative recreation was breaking glass.

Gibraltar Street from Moorfields c.1905, looking towards West Bar. Snow Lane and Allen Street come in on the right. Nichols' grocer's shop stuck out into the road and formed a bottleneck which was not removed until after 1914. The trams were forced to revert to a single line. The gabled building on the left with arched windows was the warehouse of the Gibraltar Steel Works, but the lower part was occupied by shops.

A brewer's dray, probably part of the May Day Parade, on Bridge Street, just short of the junction with Corporation Street. The cementation furnaces belong to Millsands Steel Works. On May Day working horses were decorated and prizes were awarded for the best turn-out. Even the tramcars, in horse drawn days, took part.

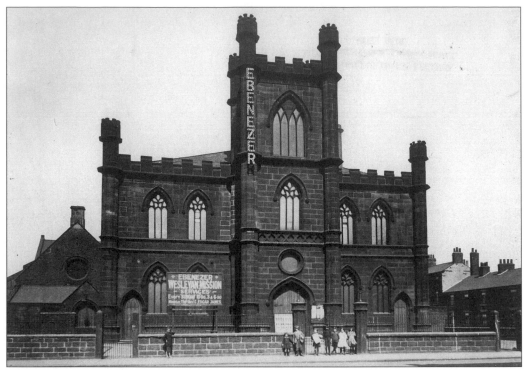

Ebenezer Wesleyan Chapel, Ebenezer Place, Shalesmoor, c.1910. The Chapel opened in 1823 and, with its schools in 1831, it became a religious and cultural centre of this growing industrial and working class district. It had iron-framed Gothic windows befitting its industrial surroundings. Originally it had a wooden spire which was considered frivolous and later removed. It is now a warehouse.

Shalesmoor c.1909, looking towards town. Dunfields is on the left, Matthew Street on the right. There was an almost uninterrupted line of small shops on both sides as far as the Town Centre. The Ship Inn on the left survives in rebuilt form.

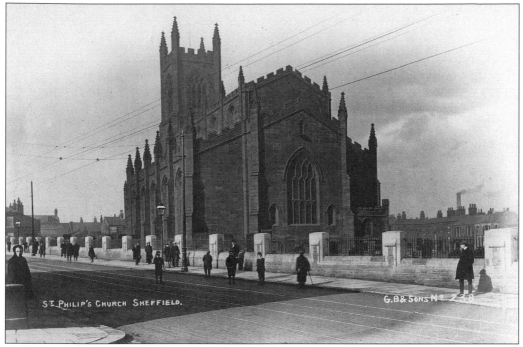

St Philip's Church from Infirmary Road, looking towards Hillsborough, c.1910. Built from the million pounds raised for Anglican churches under the Act of 1818, St Philip's opened in 1828 and gave its name to the suburb which sprang up around it. In Victorian times it was noted for its Cathedral type services and its social and educational work. It was closed in 1940 and demolished in 1952.

Eye clinic day at the Royal Infirmary outpatients' waiting room, 1897. The General Infirmary opened in 1797 and was still dependent upon charitable support. The Rotunda Building was provided for the outpatients in 1884 and has been retained as part of the Norwich Union offices. Eye trouble was a constant hazard in the vicinity of metal working shops.

Mrs Sarah Ann Bingham with family and staff outside her beerhouse, 13 Bower Street, some time in the 1890s. John Smith's beer was brewed then as now in Tadcaster, brought to Sheffield by rail and distributed from a store at Wicker Goods Station. In the 1890s it competed with twenty Sheffield-based breweries. The photograph was passed down through Ellen Gillott, who is on the back row and had unhappy memories of going to Mrs Bingham as a poor relation and being treated as a skivvy. One suspects the twins could have got away with murder.

Eleven

The Park

The medieval Lords of Sheffield preserved some 2,500 acres to the south east of the town as a deer park. It reached almost to the walls of the Castle, and originally included most of the lower Sheaf Valley. In 1637 the Park was described as "very well adorned with great store of very stately timber" and the number of deer was estimated at one thousand. By then hunting was nearly at an end and once the deer had gone the Lords turned their attention to maximizing revenue. The underground treasure of the Park included coal and ironstone, and by the eighteenth century it was divided into small farms interspersed with mineral working, with here and there the odd ruin or line of trees to recall former glories. By 1850 the Park was an area of stark contrasts. Park Hill was made up of old quarries, untidy waste ground, steep alleyways and some of the worst slums in Sheffield. Only a short distance away the Duke of Norfolk had reclaimed some industrial land to landscape a private park, in the Victorian rather than the medieval sense. The approach roads were sparingly lined with dignified middle class houses, while the leafiest corner was reserved for his own use when inspecting his Sheffield properties. In the 1960s the slums were replaced by Sheffield's most spectacular and widely applauded experiments in vertical living; fortunately Park residents have been long hardened to climbing stairs.

Bernard Street in the Park, about 1935. In the poorer and hillier end of the Park there were many streets built as terraces and linked by steep alleys or staircases like School Hill on the right. Note the men and dog huddled against the railings and Joseph Marlow's corner shop, which sold sweets and tobacco.

Court 5, Duke Street, Park, July 1926. House no 4 is on the left, with the girl on the step. House no 5 is up the steps and no 6 is on the right. Six adults and two children lived in these single room dwellings, which were not common in Sheffield outside the Park District. The people appear to be preparing to move out, probably to the new Wybourn Estate further up the hill. The Courts of the Park were breeding grounds for the senior and junior Park Gangs which terrorized the City Centre after dark. Though the Sheffield Police deserve and took credit for breaking up the gangs, dispersal of the communities from crowded slums to the suburbs must have contributed.

Opposite: Single room dwellings, Court 5, High Street Lane, Park in July 1926. No 2, up the steps, was occupied by four people. The picture was taken by the Medical Officer when the property was due for demolition.

129

A faded photograph of the cricket match between All England and Hallam and Staveley, 6 to 8 September 1858, almost the last major match to be played at Hyde Park Ground. Hyde Park opened in 1826 and was soon Sheffield's premier cricket ground, but after 1854 it suffered almost immediate eclipse by Bramall Lane. It remained popular with some local clubs and for pigeon shooting, rabbit coursing and pedestrian handicaps. In 1886 it became a drill ground for the Hallamshire Rifles.

Much of the varied sporting life of the Park escaped the camera. In the case of dog fighting and pitch-and-toss this was no accident. Mr Gillott, on the right, and his friends, hold their dog back from investigating the cameraman, c.1890.

Whit Sings in Norfolk Park, Whit Monday, 1893, with the weather for once holding up. After 1857 Norfolk Park was the main destination for the Whit Walks, the great event of the Sunday School year and a chance to show off new frocks and bonnets. The conductor is Dr Henry Coward, a cutler who rose to become a headmaster and was subsequently knighted for his service to choral music.

Preparations under way for the greatest demonstration seen in Norfolk Park, the reception of Queen Victoria on 21 May 1897. Fifty thousand children from ninety-two schools formed a welcoming choir, supported by eight brass bands. It is thought to be one of the largest choirs ever assembled. A new drive was constructed for the Queen, and the serious looking crash barriers will be noted.

Broad Street, Park, with a procession from St John's Anglican Church Sunday School in the 1890s. They are probably on their way to or from a demonstration in Norfolk Park.

The Park Picture Palace, South Street in 1917. Newsreels from the war are advertised. The initials SPP stand for Sheffield Park Palace.

The staff of the Park Picture Palace in front of the main entrance, South Street, in 1917. The cinema opened in 1913 at the lower end of the Park and had seats for 900. Wooden seats might be had for twopence, while upholstery cost fourpence or sixpence according to position. At the depth of the war the staff included Mr Keaton, in the trilby, on the back row, Percy Brothwell, the projectionist on the left and Gladys Brothwell next to him. An orchestra was also maintained. The cinema escaped the wholesale redevelopment of Park Hill, but closed in 1966. Its site is now swallowed up in the Sheaf Roundabout.

Mr Charles Green, artist and designer, in his studio at 18 Shrewsbury Road, 1910. He is shown
with his bust of Arthur Benton, Master of the Sheffield Arts Crafts Guild, which Charles Green
had founded. Charles Green (1836-1916) was a link with the golden age when Alfred Stevens
and Godfrey Sykes had raised the level of industrial design in Sheffield. He carved a font for the
Parish Church, but his most famous work was a cabinet in the fifteenth-century Italian style
made of mahogany, ebony and bronze. In his younger days he was one of the School of Art
Engineers and may be among those shown on page 140.

The Shrewsbury Hospital on Norfolk Road, c.1905. It retains its atmosphere of almost monastic calm, which in those days must have been a startling contrast with the teeming and squalid courts a little way down the hill. The original bequest to build almshouses for men and women "reduced by misfortune" was made in 1616. The Norfolk Road buildings were replacements in 1827 for ones near the River Sheaf which suffered from flooding.

The Victorian lodge on Norfolk Park Road being used as a background to display the latest Corporation motor buses. No 7 on the left was brand new in May 1913. The Tramways Department seems to have enjoyed posing its new machines in rural corners which they never reached in regular service. The few residents of Norfolk Park Road were nearly all agents or professional advisors to the Duke.

In a leafy corner of the Park, near the bottom of Granville Road, stood the Farm, a comparatively modest dwelling transformed in 1856-8 into a residence fit for the Duke of Norfolk, who had resolved to spend more time on his Sheffield estates.

An unusual navvy's eye view of the Farm during construction of the Queen's Road flyunder for the Midland Railway, 1902. In 1870, when the line first came, it hid itself from the Ducal gaze in a tunnel. With proposed new works virtually sapping his foundations, the Duke decided to lease the Farm to the railway. It remained railway offices, known to railwaymen as the Kremlin, until demolished in 1967.

Twelve

The West End

By the early nineteenth century the term West End had been established to describe the approaches to that most desirable of residential suburbs, Broomhill. The Glossop turnpike road in 1819 added a third route to the ancient alternatives of Broad Lane and Portobello. The fortunes of the new West Street were at first mixed; it was an important steel making area and some unimproved cutlery workshops can still be seen, as on page 138. More dignified buildings appeared in a piecemeal way. The largest, the Royal Hospital, closed in 1981 and its demolition has left an unsightly gap. Between Broad Lane and Portobello, St George's Church was built in 1825. It was the first of Sheffield's Million Act churches and, like the others, was built on the edge of the town and attracted a fashionable congregation. It retains a dignified precinct, thanks more to the University and Jessop's Hospital than to prosperous residents. University students now inhabit the shell of the Church. By the early years of the present century surgeons and dentists had their consulting rooms on the east end of Glossop Road and the Georgian residences of Brookhill were already overlooked by the red brick towers of the new Civic University.

Photographers on West Street recording trams squeezing through the Tudor Arch built to celebrate Edward VII's opening of the University in 1905. Bailey Lane is on the right and the shop on the near corner was familiar until recently as Morton's Cutlery Shop.

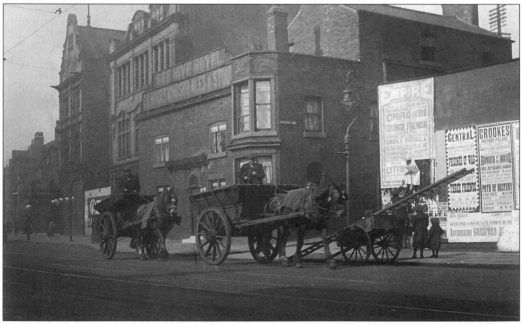

The Beehive on West Street before rebuilding, 1916. Thomas Rose, a shoemaker and amateur beekeeper, lost most of his garden when the Glossop turnpike road was built in 1819. As a compensation for his bees, the Trustees backed his application for a licence.

138

Staff at the Royal Hospital, West Street, c.1910. The Matron is Miss Annie Louisa Earle, the first Sheffield woman to fly a plane, who was to give distinguished war service in the Middle East. The men look rather left out of things.

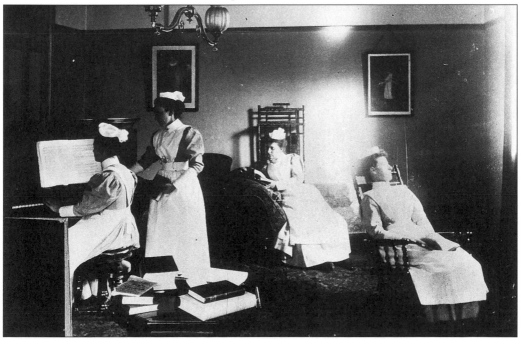

Nurses' rest room at the Royal Hospital, probably from the same official album. The literature on display looks improving. The Royal Hospital grew out of the Public Dispensary of 1832. It was demolished in 1981.

West Street seen from Fitzwilliam Street, from a postcard c.1910. The view is towards town, with the dome of the Royal Hospital prominent on the right hand side. The hoardings on the left hide building operations.

The Sheffield Royal Engineer Volunteers, probably at their first depot on Convent Walk, c.1865. They were established in 1860 in connexion with the Sheffield College of Art. The first captain was the headmaster, Young Mitchell. The theodolite and the plumbline certainly appear mightier than the sword.

Brookhill, looking towards town, c.1907. The photographer would now be standing in the middle of the roundabout. St George's Church is on the right and beyond it the first (1904) stage of the familiar Applied Science Buildings on Mappin Street.

The companion postcard to the one above, looking towards Broomhill from a few hundred yards nearer town; Brightmore Place on the right still stands. The new University, red brick and fortress-like, crowns the skyline. Ultimately it was to engulf all the Georgian houses seen in the distance.

Mr and Mrs John Hayball, Mr and Mrs Thomas Hayball and Mrs Hannah Hayball with her daughters Edith, Miriam and Laura on the backsteps of 50 (later 112) Hanover Street. Hannah's husband Arthur was the photographer and if the shot was taken soon after he moved to Hanover Street in 1853 it must be the oldest in the book. Arthur Hayball (1823-1887) was a skilled woodcarver who specialised in cabinets in various historical styles together with church furniture, which was equally in demand for Anglican restorations and new Roman Catholic churches. A walnut cabinet of his was exhibited at the Crystal Palace in 1851 and his work can be seen locally at Ecclesfield Parish Church and in St Marie's Cathedral. He had his own workshop in the garden at Hanover Street and was interested in photography primarily to record his work. He could send prints to potential customers at home and overseas. Portraits and views were an occasional sideline, and the earliest examples, like the one opposite, were often taken from upstairs windows.

Allotments at the back of Hanover Street, looking towards Broomspring Lane, c.1856. Growing fruit and vegetables was popular with all classes. Note the flower pot extensions to the garden house chimney, and the stack of old crucible pots, which, bottoms removed, served to force celery or rhubarb. Towards Broomspring Lane the surface clay has been removed for brick-making, pending building.

Broomhall Road was the carriage drive to the exclusive Broomhall Park, but Victorian development turned out decidedly mixed. Mrs Anne Pashley, at no 104 on the left, was officially a licensed dealer in marine stores, more particularly defined in her notice. The Broomhall Flats were later built across this part of the street.

Gell Street, at the corner of Broomspring Lane, c.1905. The building behind the tree is the Servants' Home, which was used between 1886 and 1931 to train respectable girls for domestic service. It freed orphan girls from the "taint" of coming from the Workhouse and provided a home for them to turn to when sick or out of work.

Reuben Thompson's coach and cab office at the corner of Glossop Road and Upper Hanover Street, c.1905, with a hansom and growler on the stand. The large gable on the left belonged to his multi-storey stables, which provided horses for his coaching, hackney carriage and funeral business.

Thirteen

Cutlery, Edge Tools, Silver Plate

Engravings were made of the traditional Sheffield trades from early in the nineteenth century, but few photographs were taken before 1900. The cramped and ill-lit workshops in the town centre presented a challenge to early cameras. After 1900 several of the larger firms commissioned photographs of their workers. Traditional skills and hand craftwork were important selling points, especially at the upper end of the American market. Some of the photographs on the following pages were used in a brochure for the Suffolk Works, Suffolk Street, in 1903, when the owner, A.J. Hobson, was Master Cutler. The pictures were not necessarily taken there, as many firms sub-contracted specialised work to little mesters who rented their own premises. Another set was taken by Mottershaws for Needham Veall and Tyzack, Eye Witness Works, Milton Street. The photographs of plate workers were used in Frederick Bradbury's *History of Old Sheffield Plate* in 1912 and were probably taken at the family works, though it seems strange that he should draw attention to an apparent breach of contemporary safety regulations.

By 1900 there were a number of large works in the City Centre, and cutlery and plate were often produced on the same premises, which would have been unthinkable fifty years earlier. Impressive façades and imposing names nevertheless often belied primitive working conditions and the skilled worker was often earning less than his or her counterpart in 1850.

Double forging pick blades at an unknown location, c.1900. Heavy work like this required co-ordination between the forger (on the left) and his striker. Increasingly, the striker's place was being taken by machinery. Note the variety of anvils in use.

Old Henry Martin hand forging saw files, c.1902. This photograph was used for the Suffolk Works brochure. The photographer had by then tactfully touched in the missing brick. Larger files were forged by machine, but with the smaller sizes you could, as the brochure pointed out, "still admire the dexterity of the forger who shapes the heated steel with a hammer which seems to respond as easily to his wishes as a brush would do in the hands of an artist."

Old Kirk and William Carr are seen goffing table knife blades, 1902. Old Kirk and his more modern machine featured in the Suffolk Works brochure to illustrate the advance of machine forging. This took the hard slog out of the job and 1500 dozen table blades a week could be produced this way. As the brochure commented, "generally speaking machine processes are good enough for ordinary table blades provided the quality of the steel used is what it should be."

Filing the rough edges off scissor handles at Needham Veall and Tyzack, Milton Street, c.1905. This was regarded as the less skilled part of silver manufacture; note that there are women at work in the background. Scissor blades started with the forger, but the greatest skill had to be exercised in assembling. The first task of the scissor-maker was to put the two blades together and bore a hole for the screw. This had to be in three sizes to allow the upper blade to turn and to countersink the head. The two blades then had to be heated and tempered together to ensure they were of equal hardness. The most skilled job of all was setting. Each blade had to be hollow from rivet to point and back to edge, so as to touch at one point only. This task was carried out with a hammer, judging by sight alone.

A scissor maker at work, possibly at E.M. Oakes and Co., Solly Street, though he was used to illustrate the Suffolk Works brochure in 1902. He is setting the blades. Note the bowler hat on the hook, ready for the journey home.

John Henry Simpson, left, setting saw teeth at Suffolk Works, 1902. Setting consisted of bending teeth alternately in opposite directions at exactly the same angle, using a hammer and a stake bevelled at the correct angle. This called for great dexterity in the case of small saws with 18 or 24 teeth to the inch. On the right each tooth is being sharpened, possibly using one of the files Henry Martin has been shown forging on page 146. A skilled sawmaker would then be earning 30 to 40 shillings a week, which was actually somewhat less than his counterpart in the heyday of the trade in the 1840s. The vast majority of saws had long been set by machine.

A cutlery shop c.1905, where buffing and finishing processes are being undertaken by men. Buffing wheels hang in racks. The Medical Officer of Health was responsible for taking this picture, the batswing gas burners being particular objects of attention.

Old Clegg using a bow saw to cut out a saw handle from a solid block of wood for Thomas Turner and Wingfield Rowbotham, Suffolk Works, 1902. He was chosen to illustrate their brochure *Handicrafts that Survive*, which understandably favoured ancient and picturesque workers. The vast bulk of their manufacture was by then mechanized, and the skill of their hand workers was not really reflected in their earnings; old Clegg would have been lucky to take home 30 shillings a week.

Rivetting penknives, Needham Veall and Tyzack's Eye Witness Works, Milton Street, 1906. Assembling a penknife was regarded by many authorities as the supreme test of a craftsman. Miniscule examples were proudly presented to visiting dignitaries and others were produced with hundreds of blades. The simplest tools were required. Benches were usually placed beneath a window, but lighting was a problem; there is no sign of individual gas burners. Note the period pin-ups; the lady was presumably a music hall star.

Boring and fitting staghorn handles, Needham Veall and Tyzack's, 1906. The tang attached to the blade extended the whole length of the handle, and the best quality knives were rivetted at the end. The material was often brittle and this could be a delicate operation. The pans by the fire grate were used for making up a mixture of resin, whitening and ash from the fire, which hardened into a cement and fixed the tang into the handle. Chicken wire guards are fitted to the benches on the upper tier.

Buffer girls at work at J.G. Graves' Enterprise Works, on the corner of Shoreham Street and St Mary's Road, c.1934. They are wearing the traditional red head scarves and calico brats, but not, apparently, the equally famous paper leggings. Men buffers worked in separate shops, usually on large objects like soup tureens, but buffing was the most distinctive women's job in the Sheffield trades. The life and lore of the buffer lasses can be read in *Diamonds in Brown Paper* compiled by Gill Booth in 1988. Most buffers were organized in shops under the Missus Buffer. Girls started at 14 and were allowed on the wheels at 16. A range of objects from spoons and forks to tea pots required buffing on a leather covered wheel or a dolly made of textile, using a handful of sand and oil known as "buffing muck". This filthy concoction was unpleasant to work with and provided ample incentive to any male apprentice to steer clear of the buffing shops. By reputation buffers were a cheerful lot, and singing from the shops could be heard in the streets. For women they were relatively well paid; some brought home better wages than their husbands.

Packing and labelling cutlery for dispatch at Needham Veall and Tyzack's warehouse, Milton Street. Warehouses had long provided alternative work for girls who could read and write, but there was not much status attached. Boys starting on the same job could be promoted to the office, but this rarely happened to women before the First World War.

This commercial postcard shows women at an unknown works etching cutlery blades, c.1910. The mark or pattern was etched by applying an acid mixture through an acid resistant transfer, which had to be individually cut out and accurately laid. Note the gas lighting.

A flypunch in use c.1910, probably at Thomas Bradbury and Son's Works, Arundel Street. This invention proved a godsend for workers in Old Sheffield Plate, where it virtually replaced saw piercing. It worked by driving a shaped chisel head through a piece of plate into a correspondingly shaped die below. The beauty was that it forced the silver on the surface into the cut, instead of leaving an exposed copper edge. Here it is seen piercing an ornamental rim on a silver soy frame base. The bundle of cotton waste, according to Bradbury, should have been tied to the ends of the rotating levers to soften the blow on any passing operative.

Burnishing a silver tray at Thomas Bradbury and Son's, c.1910. Burnishing was a highly skilled job, invariably carried out by women. After degreasing the surface there were two stages to the operation. First a steel burnisher would be worked backwards and forwards with great pressure. A bluestone or bloodstone would then be used to obtain a darker colour. Burnishes had to be dipped in the sud pot to prevent their dragging the surface and would periodically need to be rubbed on a leather strop sprinkled with burnishing putty.

Walker and Hall's Electro Works on Howard Street, c.1930. This was one of the largest and most impressive cutlery and plate works and formed a landmark in the City Centre. Part of its site is now covered by the Town Hall Extensions. As the name implies, its fortune was originally made from the invention of electroplating in the 1840s, but by 1900 it had branched out into cutlery and sterling silver. A thousand workers were employed in the 1890s and the number had doubled by 1913. The credit for this expansion was claimed by Col Sir John Bingham, nephew of the founding Walker and the model of a successful plate manufacturer. The works were organised on semi-military lines, rank was strictly observed and staff and work people were forbidden to fraternize. Ambitious male employees made use of the indoor rifle range, as Sir John was a keen Volunteer and an early advocate of national service. If they survived to 65, employees could enjoy a Company pension of up to 7s. 6d. a week; this non-contributory scheme started in 1892. Sir John was a well-known figure outside the works; he had been Master Cutler twice, was a Conservative member of the Town Council, a Fair Trader who believed in Fair Trade rather than free trade (particularly in cutlery), and the scourge of Anglican clergy caught out in un-Protestant practices.

Sir John is here seen congratulating Reuben Thompson of the City Mews, Pinstone Street, on his latest acquisition, the first motor taxi-cab in Sheffield, 1905. Sir John (should there be any doubt) is on the right, and may well be on his way to or from home in Ranmoor.

Sir John used his years on the Council to promote smoke abatement (ahead of his time) and the repaving of the streets with wood instead of slippery granite. He had come a nasty cropper in Glossop Road. He also gave a park to the City and helped to save the Botanical Gardens. The fountain on the right was part of his scheme to transform the gloomy St Paul's Churchyard (which his office overlooked) into a "green oasis". Water squirted from the ferrule of the umbrella. Vandals, alas, made short work of it.

Joseph Rogers and Sons' first cutlery showroom, 6 Norfolk Street, which was replaced by a larger one in 1860. The larger manufacturers encouraged distinguished visitors, and Rogers', who boasted royal patronage, were the first to provide a special display room for their reception. It must have seemed strangely out of place within a grimy works when it opened in 1821. A few other firms copied, but after 1900 money tended to be diverted towards extravagant premises in central London and other capital cities.

The staircase to Joseph Rodgers and Sons' offices and showrooms, c.1911. The gentleman is probably Mr John Rodgers, then Managing Director, who is demonstrating the size of his giant elephant tusks. African ivory was much prized for the best mounts and handles; these tusks seemed too magnificent to cut up. Even the sweepings from ivory cutters' floors were valuable. If they were boiled in water a jelly could be skimmed off, which prize-fighters and athletes would take before contests, nervous bridegrooms sup on their wedding nights, and ladies dissolve in a little sherry and drink at tea time.